FUNGUS
The UNBEARABLE ROT of BEING

by JAMES KOCHALKA

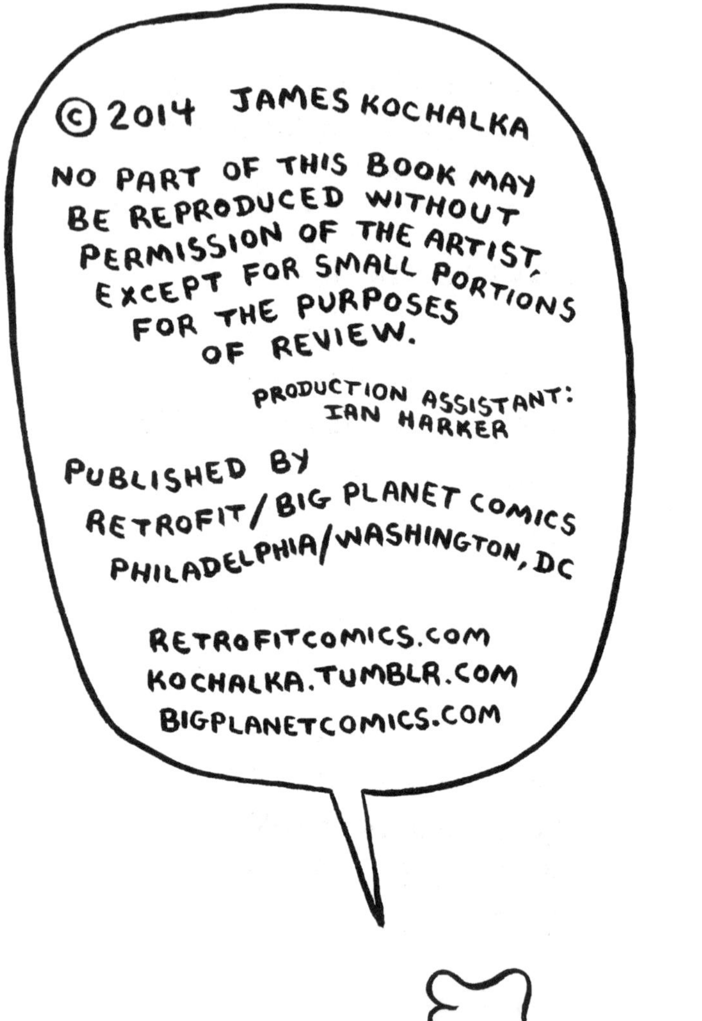
© 2014 JAMES KOCHALKA
NO PART OF THIS BOOK MAY BE REPRODUCED WITHOUT PERMISSION OF THE ARTIST, EXCEPT FOR SMALL PORTIONS FOR THE PURPOSES OF REVIEW.
PRODUCTION ASSISTANT: IAN HARKER
PUBLISHED BY RETROFIT/BIG PLANET COMICS PHILADELPHIA/WASHINGTON, DC
RETROFITCOMICS.COM
KOCHALKA.TUMBLR.COM
BIGPLANETCOMICS.COM

Other notable works
  by James Kochalka
    include:

AMERICAN ELF
 SUPERF*CKERS
FANCY FROGLIN
THE CUTE MANIFESTO
 QUIT YOUR JOB
 TINY BUBBLES
 KISSERS
FANTASTIC BUTTERFLIES
MONKEY VS. ROBOT
JOHNNY BOO
DRAGON PUNCHER
 GLORKIAN WARRIOR
 PARADISE SUCKS
 ELF CAT

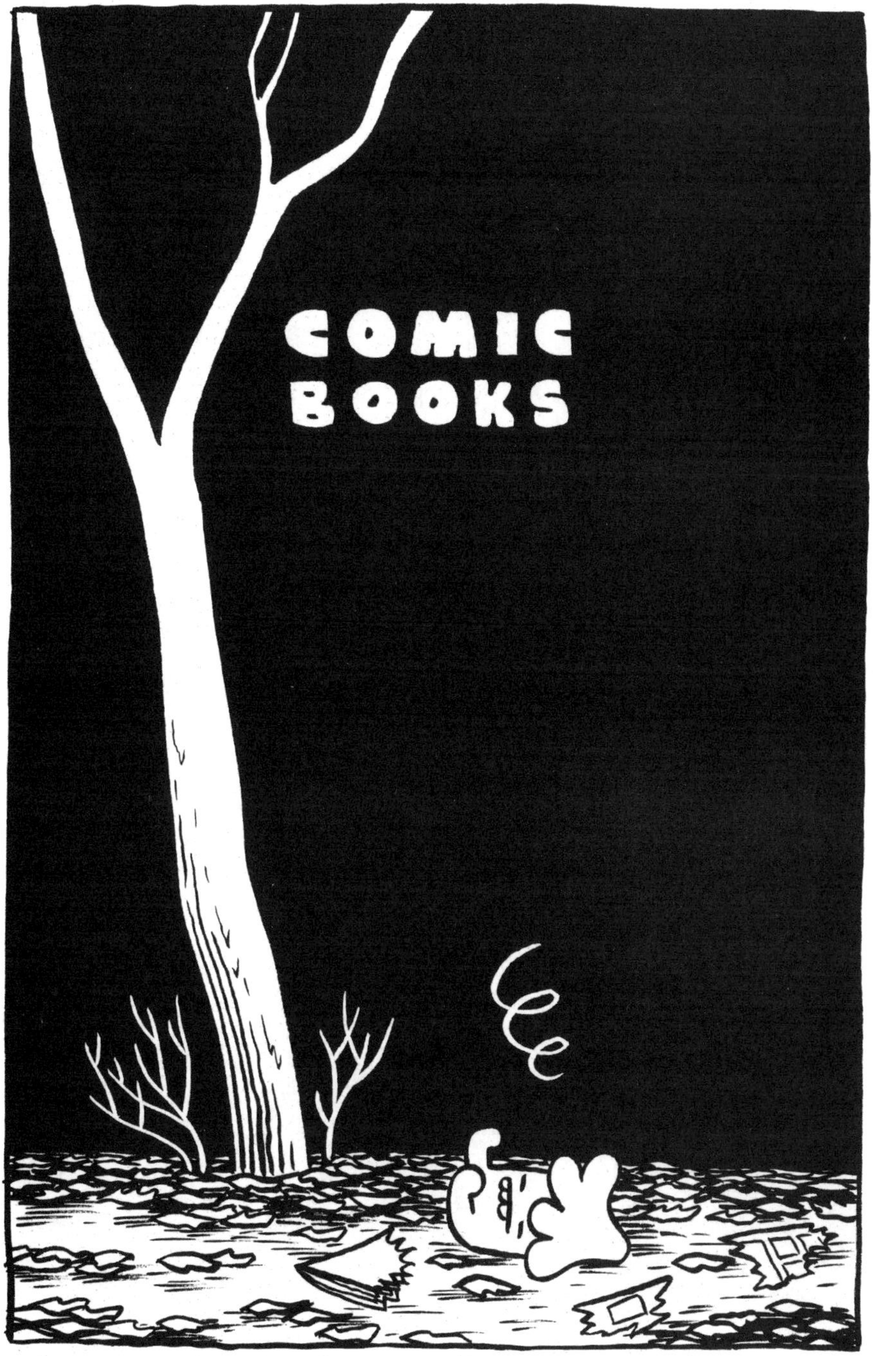
COMIC
BOOKS

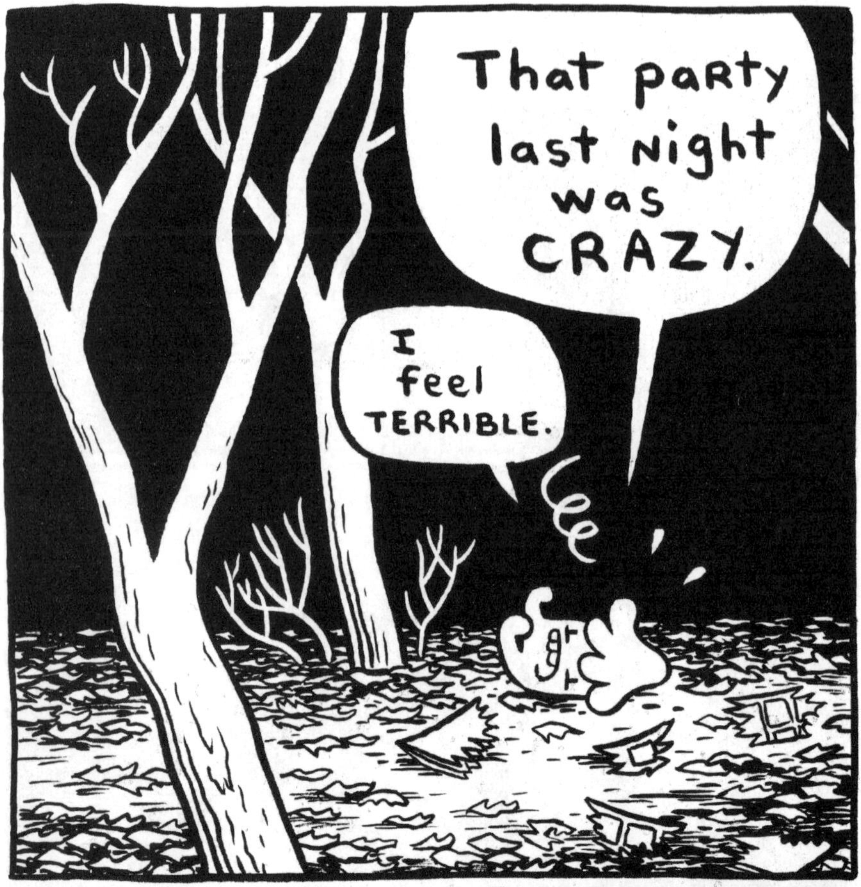
That party last night was CRAZY.
I feel TERRIBLE.

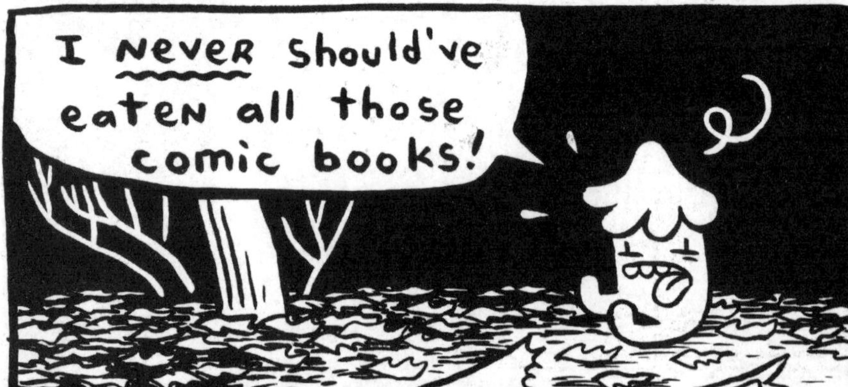
I NEVER should've eaten all those comic books!

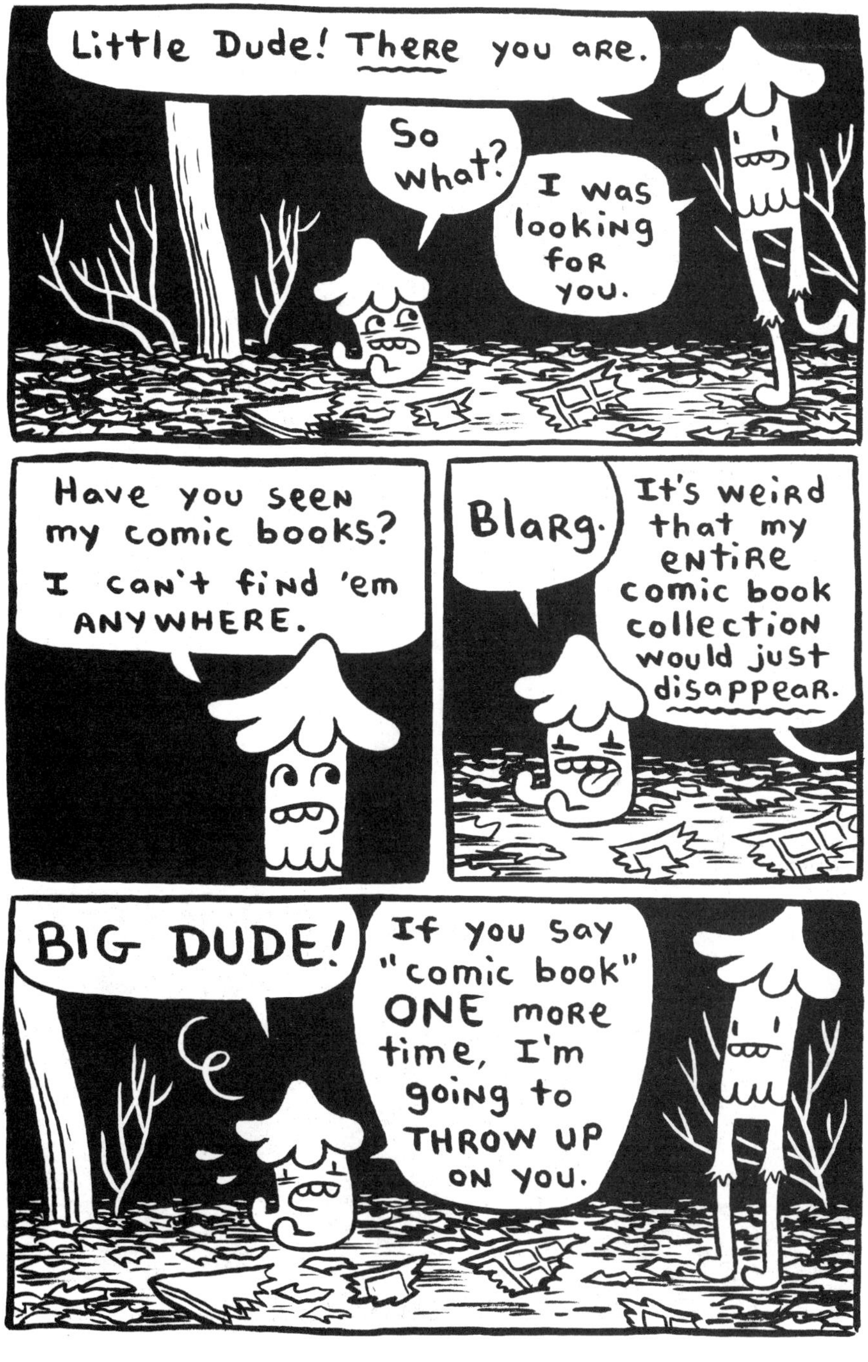
Little Dude! There you are.
So what?
I was looking for you.
Have you seen my comic books? I can't find 'em ANYWHERE.
Blarg.
It's weird that my entire comic book collection would just disappear.
BIG DUDE!
If you say "comic book" ONE more time, I'm going to THROW UP on you.

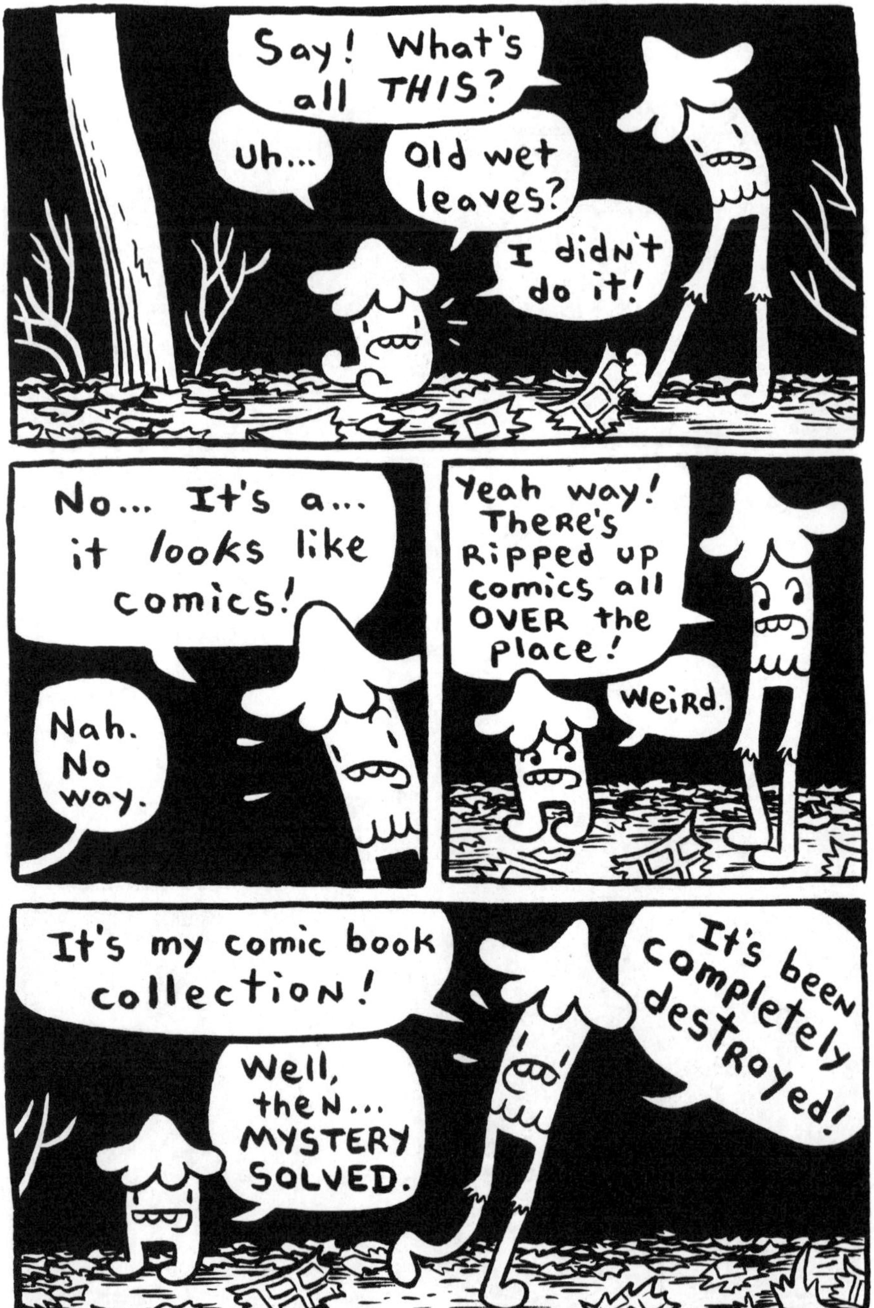
Say! What's all THIS?
Uh...
Old wet leaves?
I didn't do it!
No... It's a... it looks like comics!
Nah. No way.
Yeah way! There's ripped up comics all OVER the place!
Weird.
It's my comic book collection!
It's been completely destroyed!
Well, then... MYSTERY SOLVED.

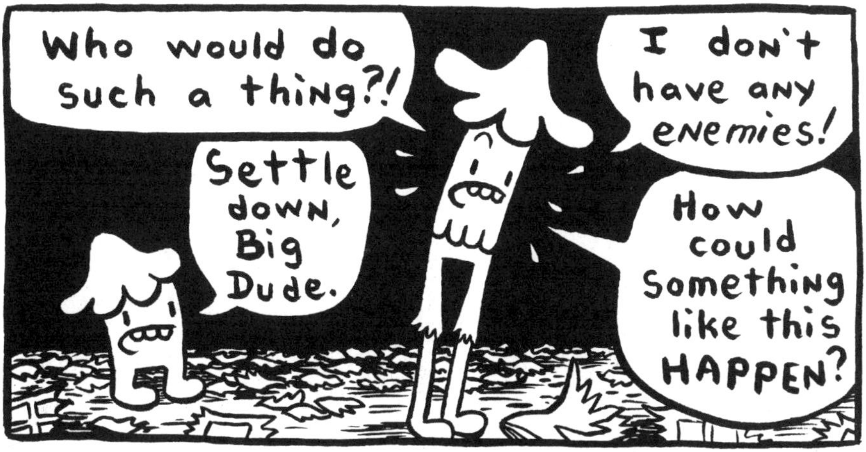
Who would do such a thing?!
I don't have any enemies!
Settle down, Big Dude.
How could something like this HAPPEN?

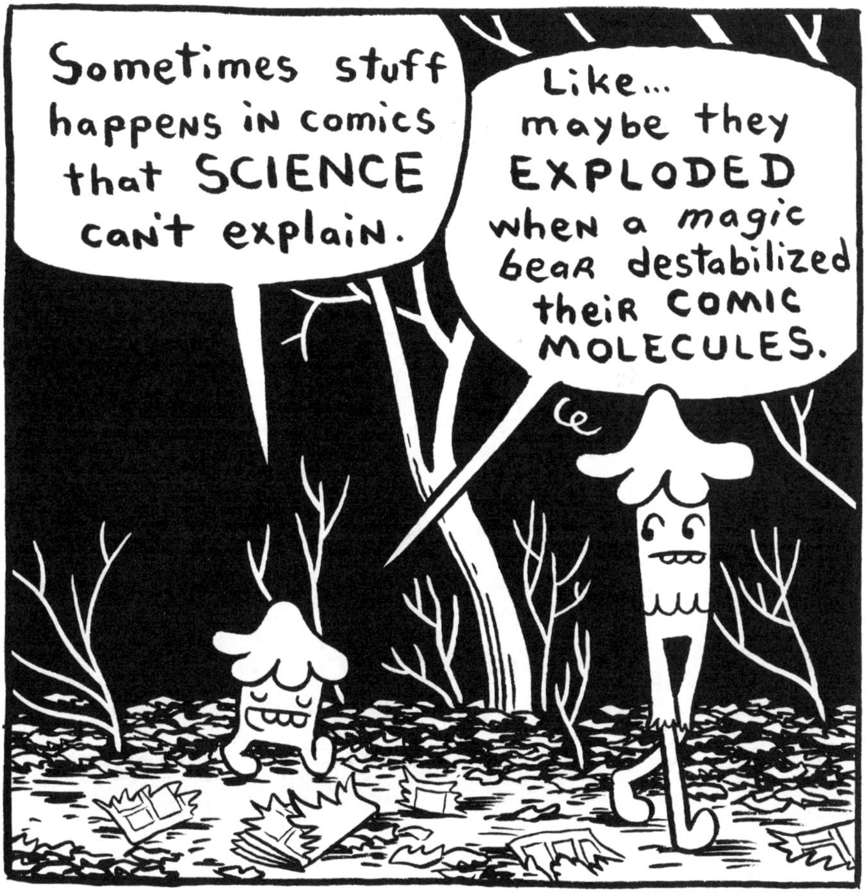
Sometimes stuff happens in comics that SCIENCE can't explain.
Like... maybe they EXPLODED when a magic bear destabilized their COMIC MOLECULES.

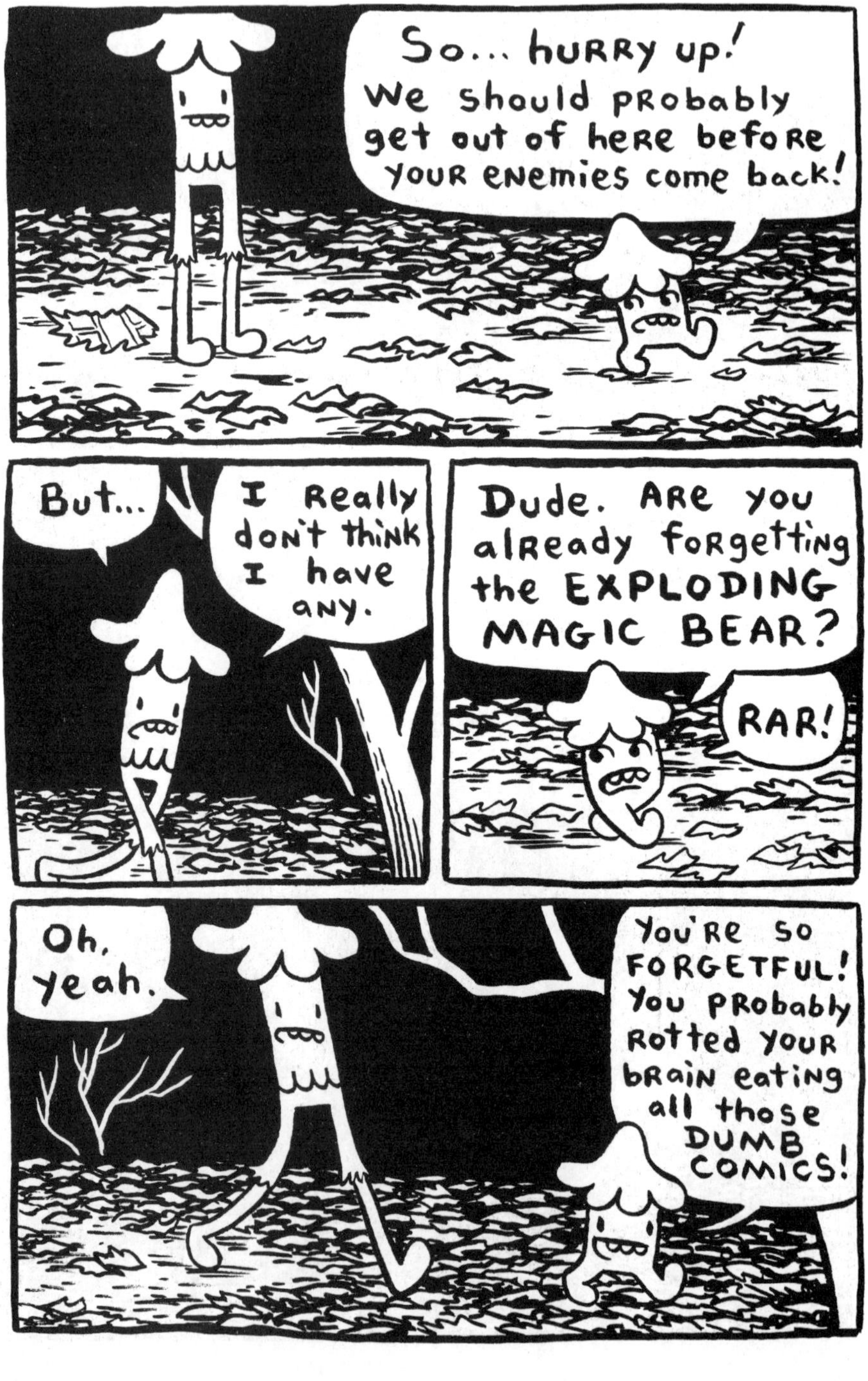
So... hurry up! We should probably get out of here before your enemies come back!
But...
I really don't think I have any.
Dude. Are you already forgetting the EXPLODING MAGIC BEAR?
RAR!
Oh, yeah.
You're so FORGETFUL! You probably rotted your brain eating all those DUMB COMICS!

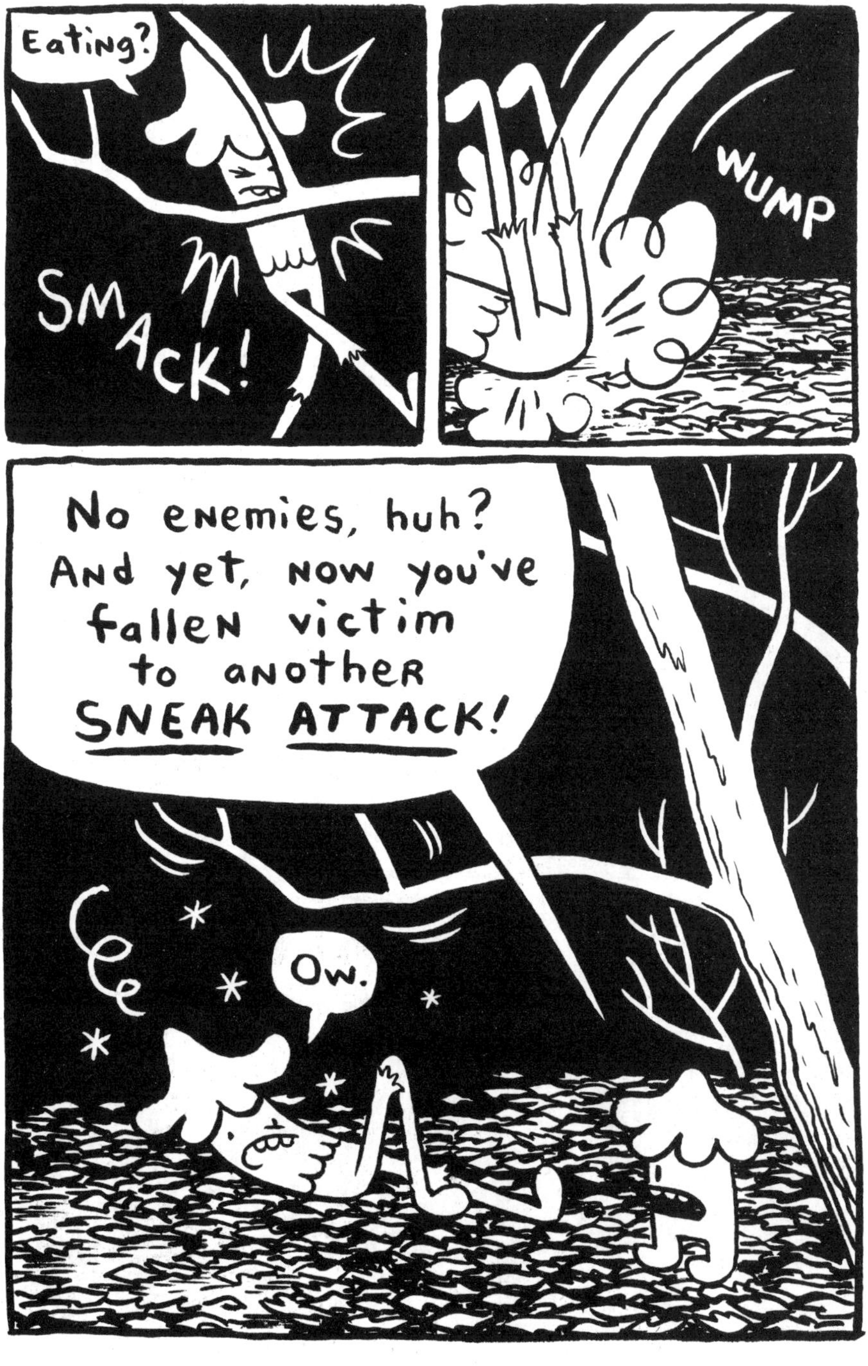
Eating?
SMACK!
WUMP
No enemies, huh? And yet, now you've fallen victim to another SNEAK ATTACK!
Ow.

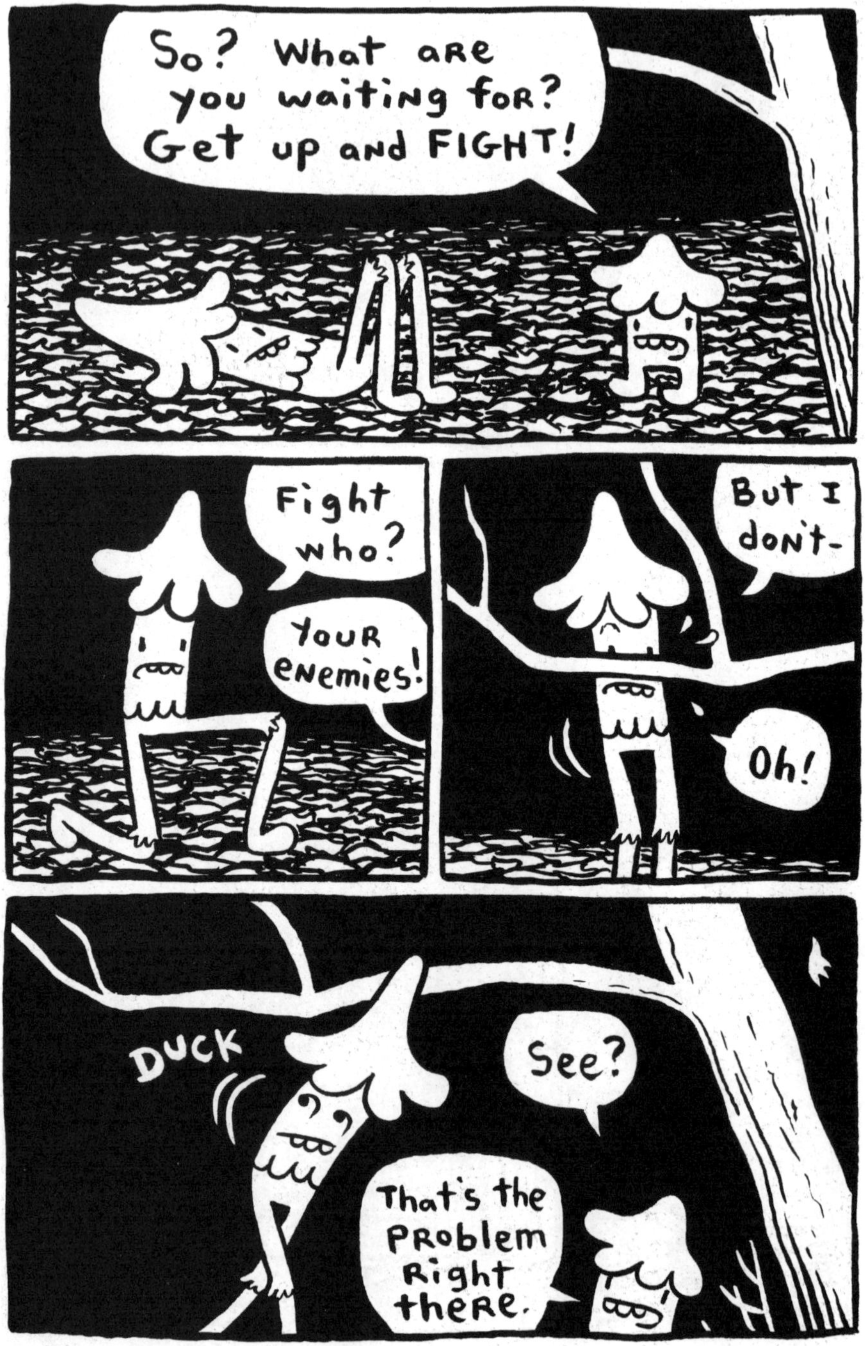
So? What are you waiting for? Get up and FIGHT!
Fight who?
Your enemies!
But I don't-
Oh!
DUCK
See?
That's the problem right there.

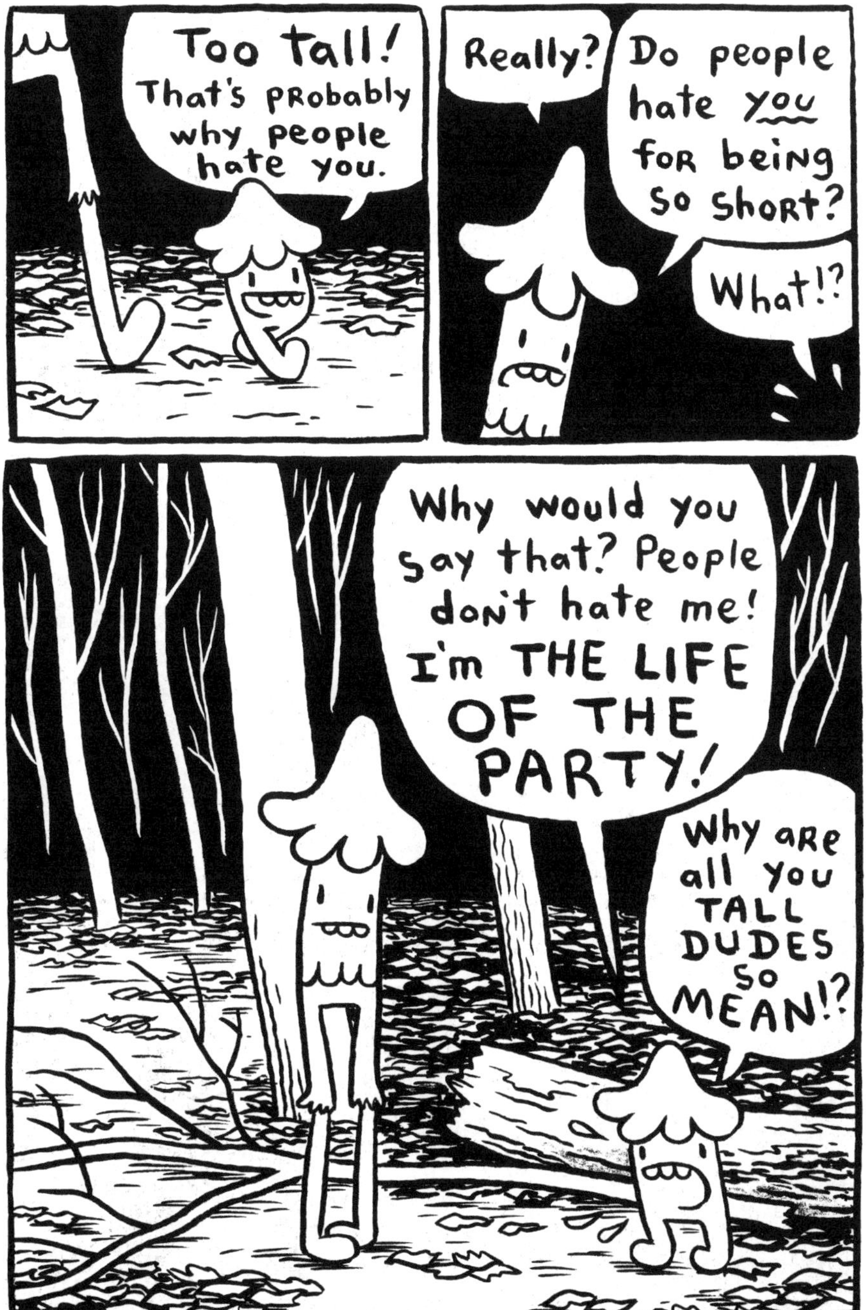
Too tall! That's probably why people hate you.
Really?
Do people hate you for being so short?
What!?
Why would you say that? People don't hate me! I'm THE LIFE OF THE PARTY!
Why are all you TALL DUDES SO MEAN!?

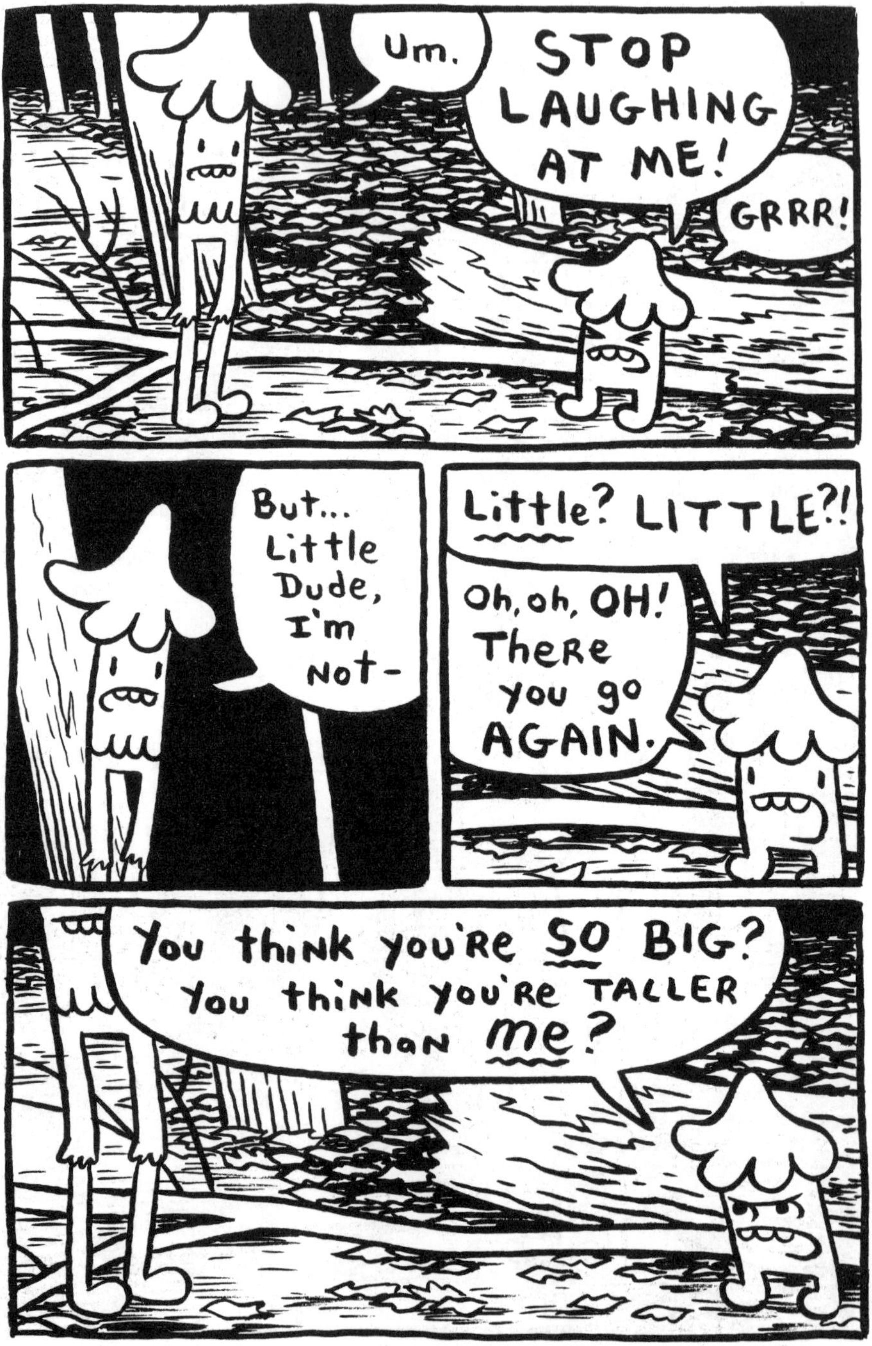
Um.
STOP LAUGHING AT ME!
GRRR!
But... Little Dude, I'm Not-
Little? LITTLE?!
Oh, oh, OH! There you go AGAIN.
You think you're SO BIG? You think you're TALLER than me?

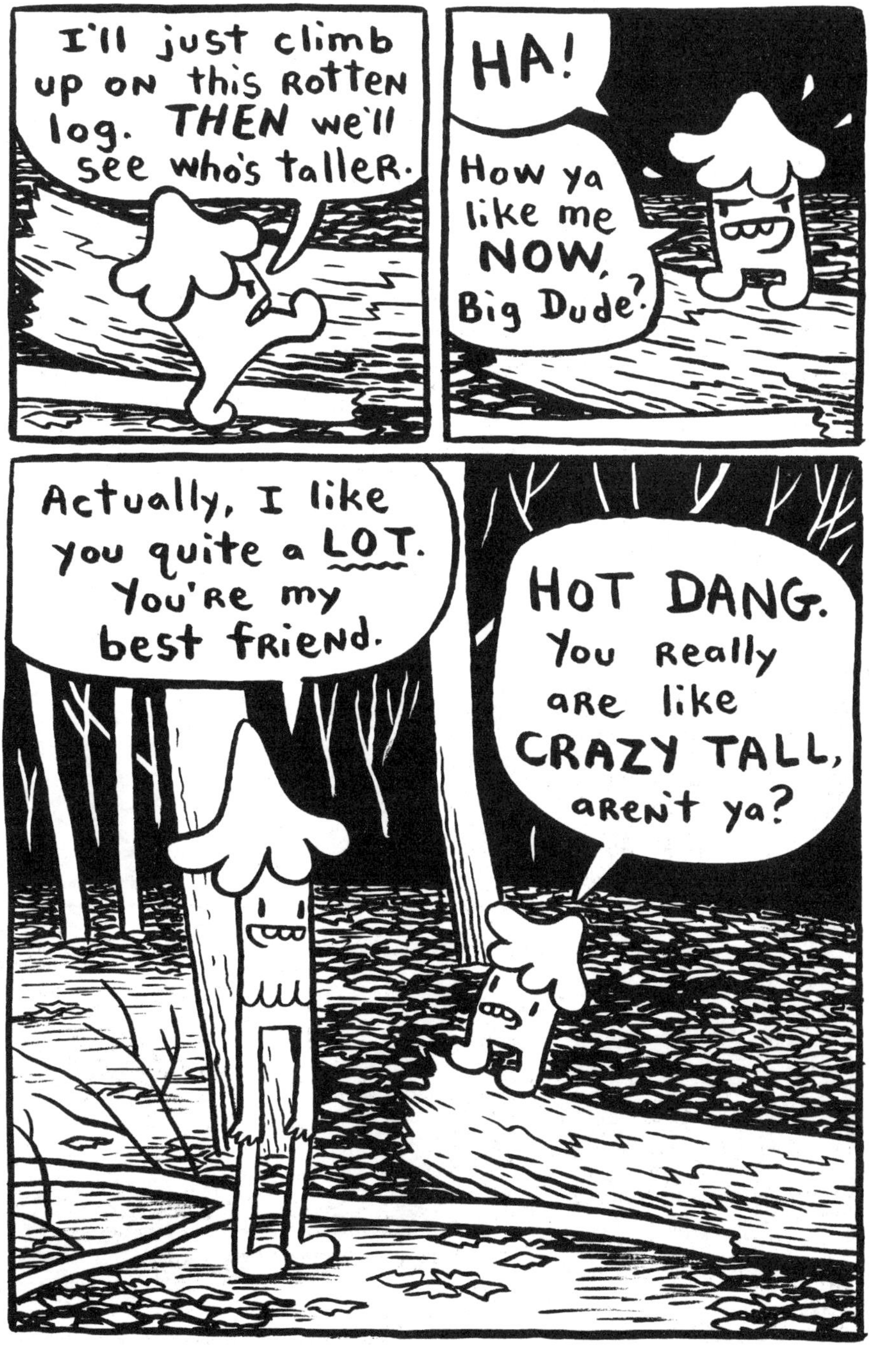
I'll just climb up on this rotten log. THEN we'll see who's taller.
HA!
How ya like me NOW, Big Dude?
Actually, I like you quite a LOT. You're my best friend.
HOT DANG. You really are like CRAZY TALL, aren't ya?

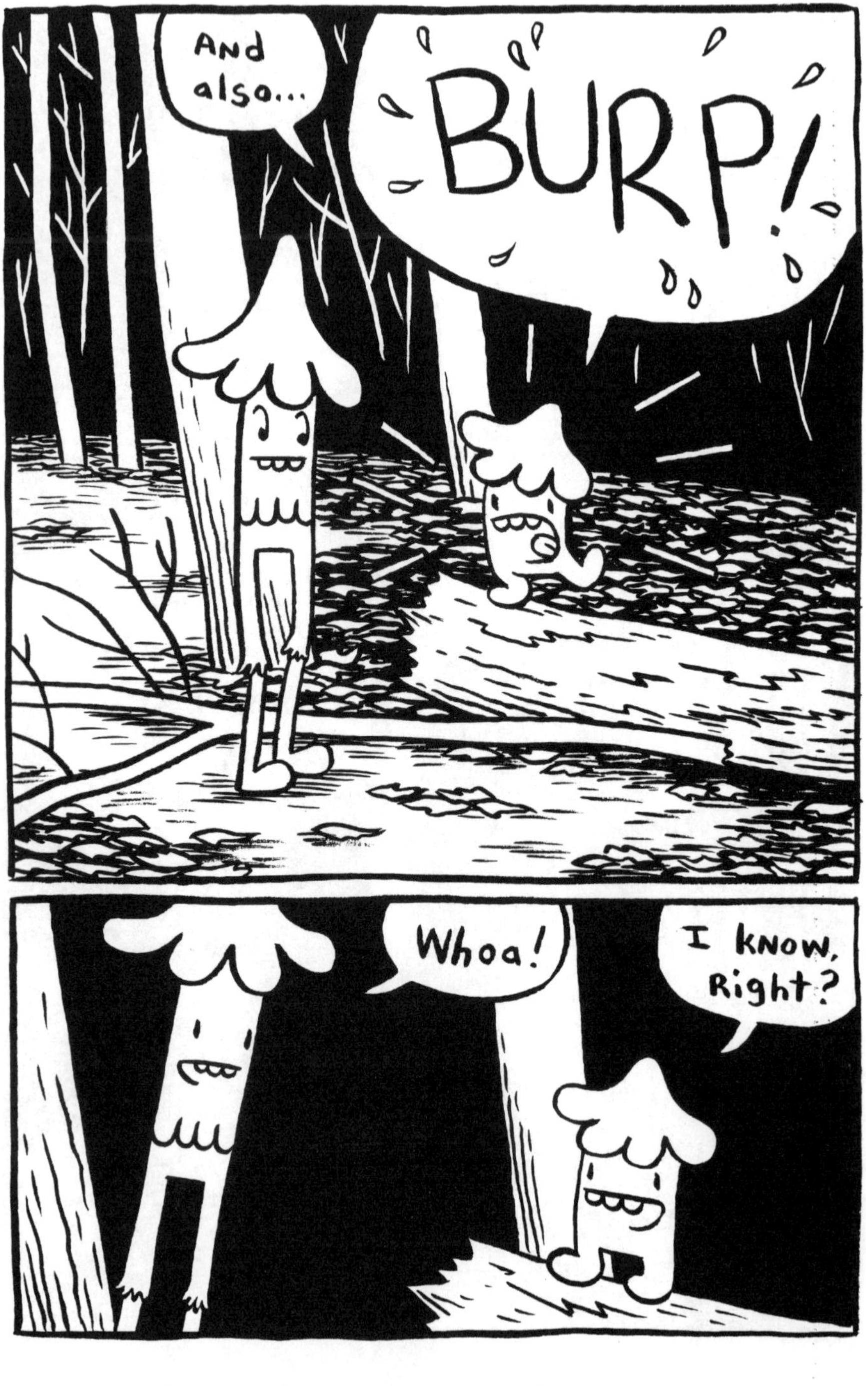
And also...
BURP!
Whoa!
I know, Right?

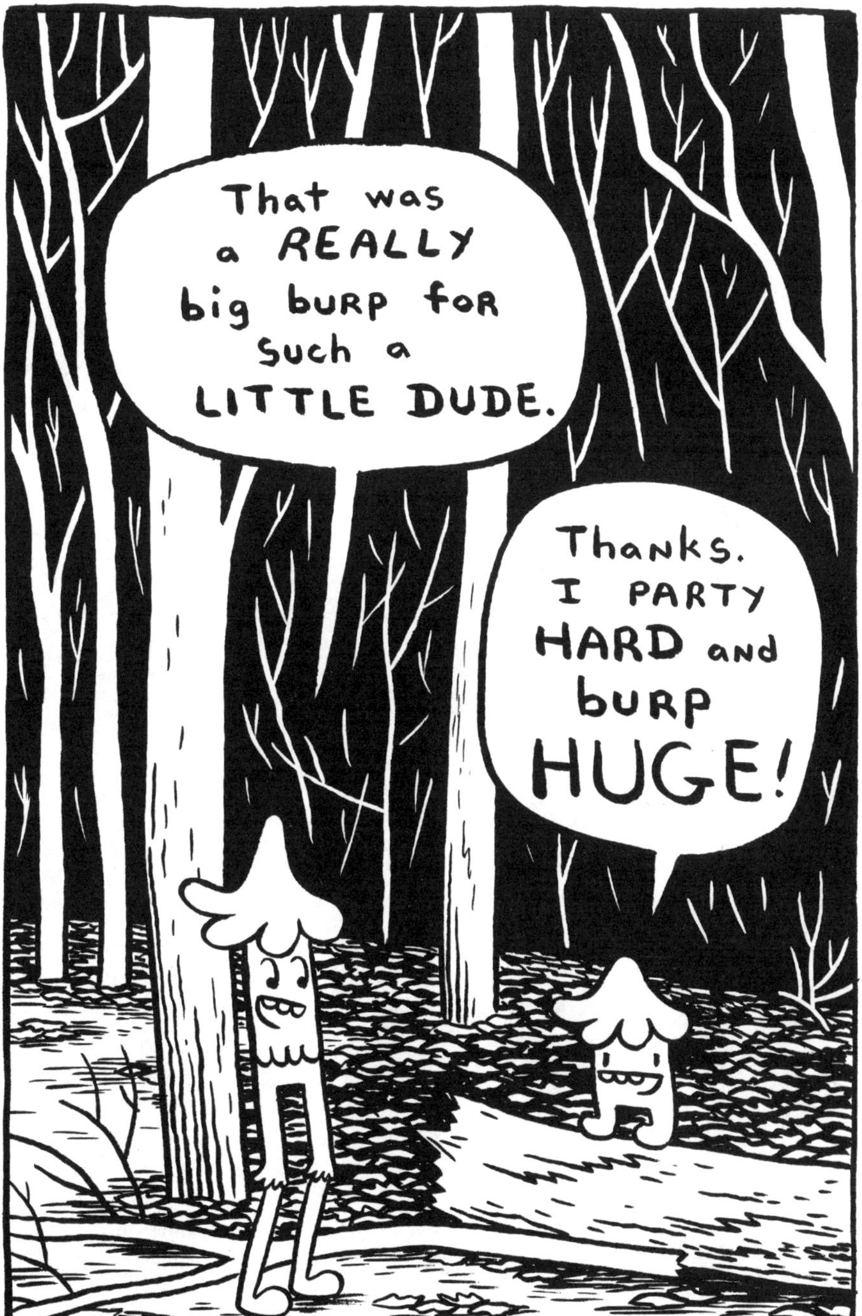
That was a REALLY big burp for such a LITTLE DUDE.
Thanks. I PARTY HARD and burp HUGE!

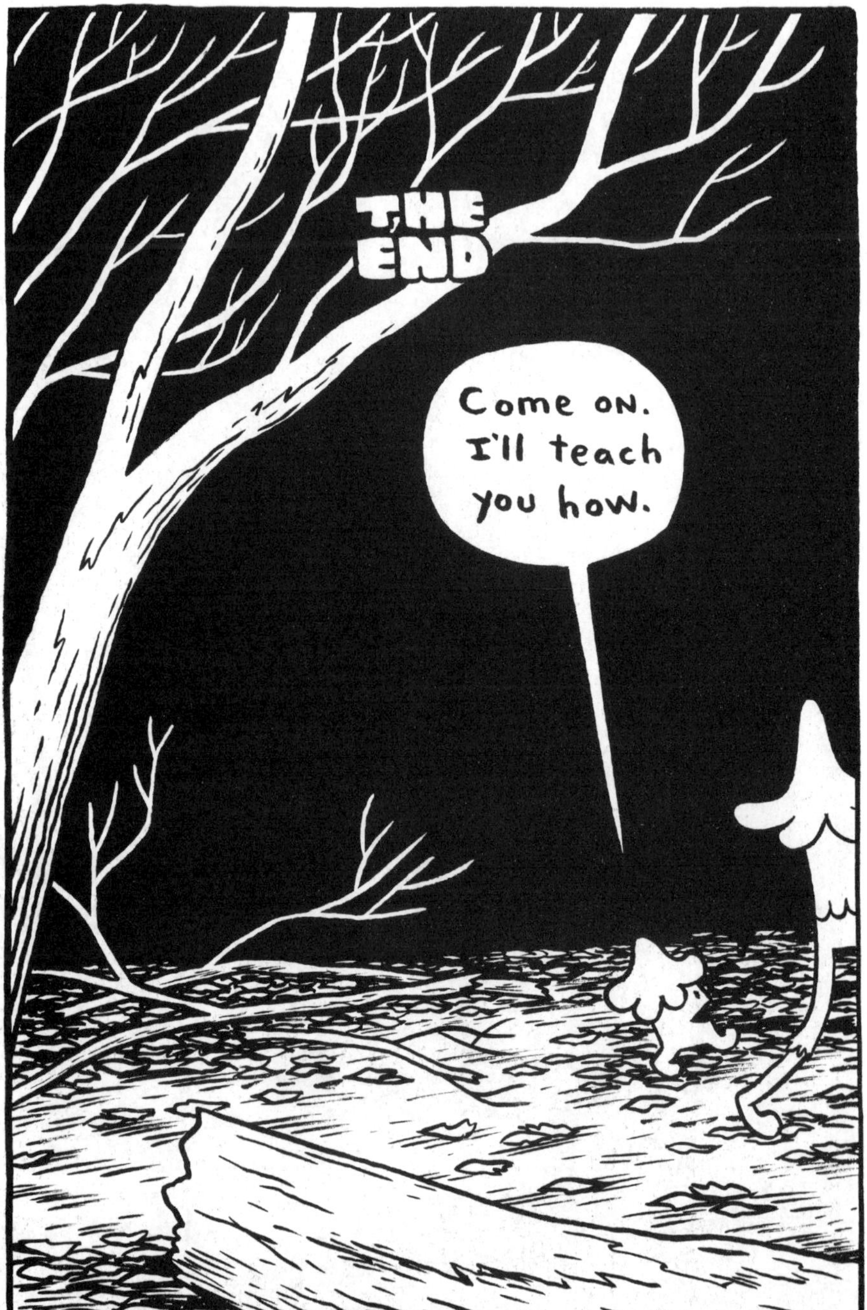
THE END
Come on. I'll teach you how.

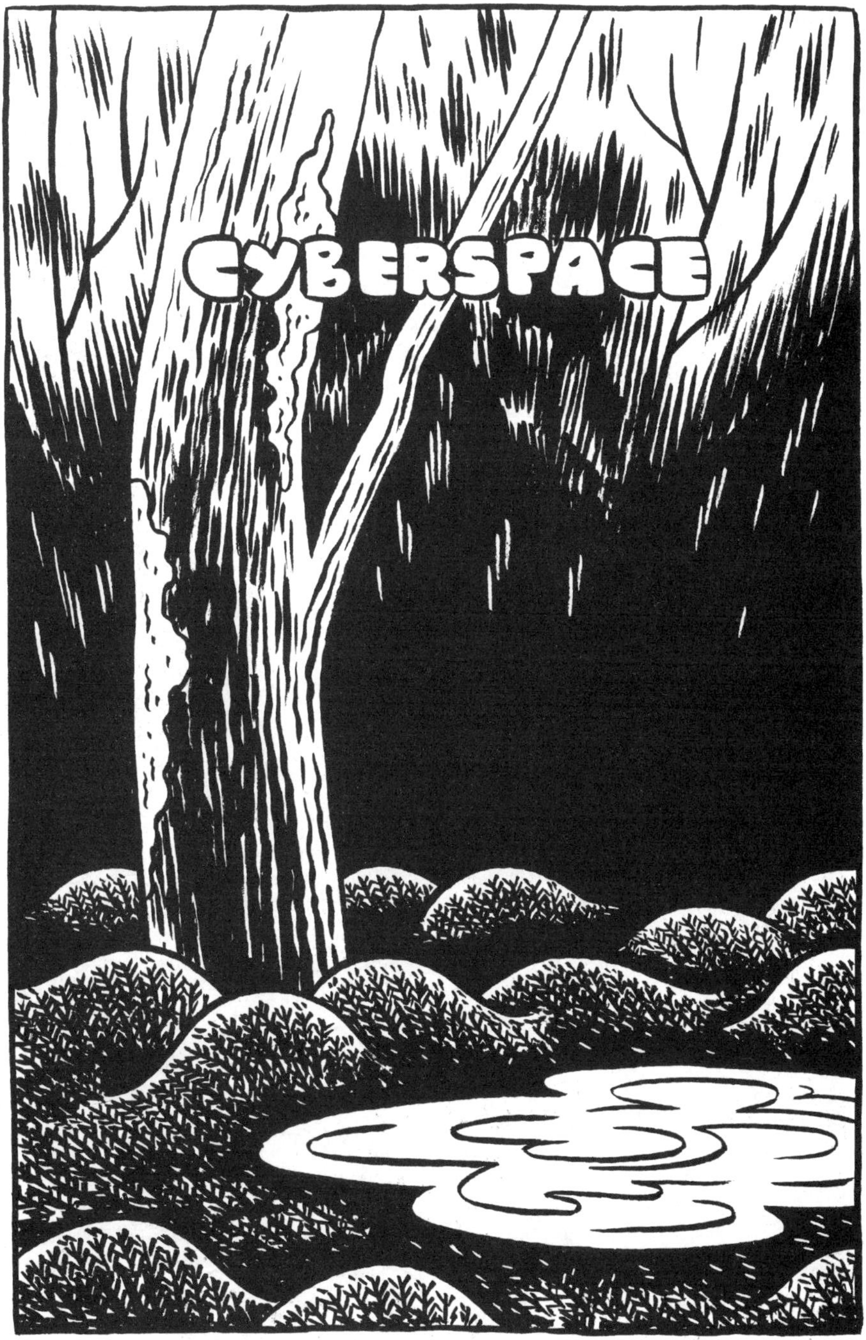
CYBERSPACE

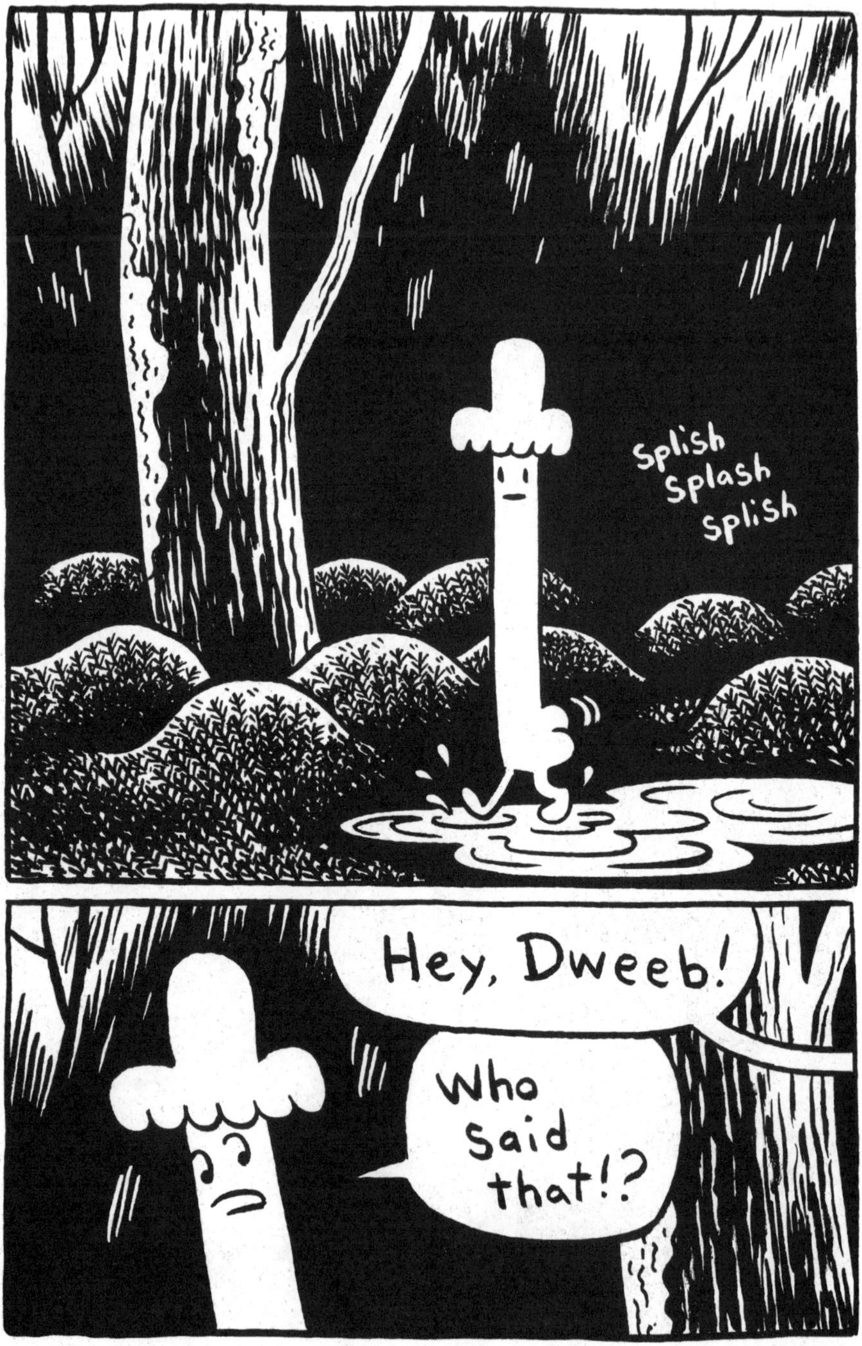
Splish
Splash
Splish
Hey, Dweeb!
Who said that!?

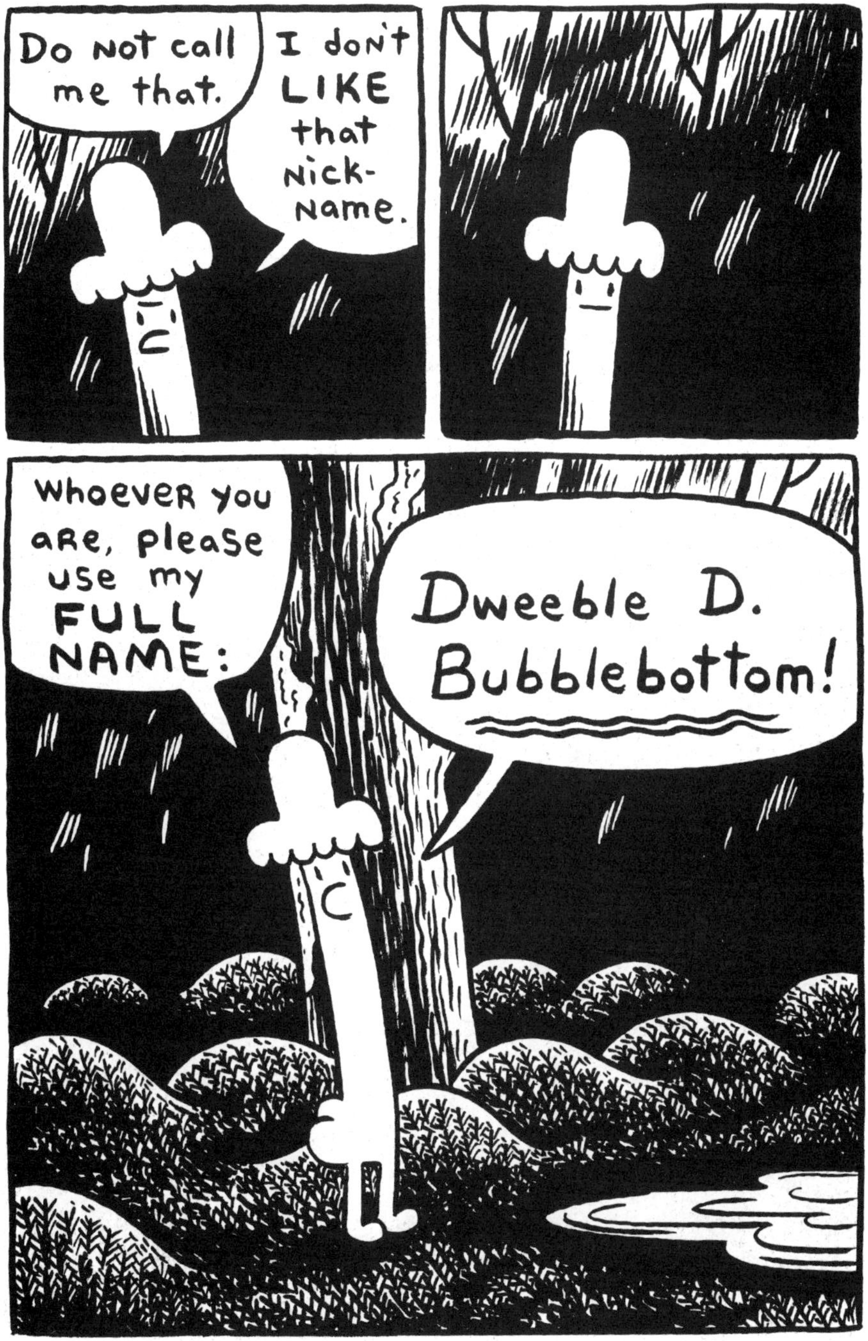
Do not call me that.
I don't LIKE that nick-name.
Whoever you are, please use my FULL NAME:
Dweeble D. Bubblebottom!

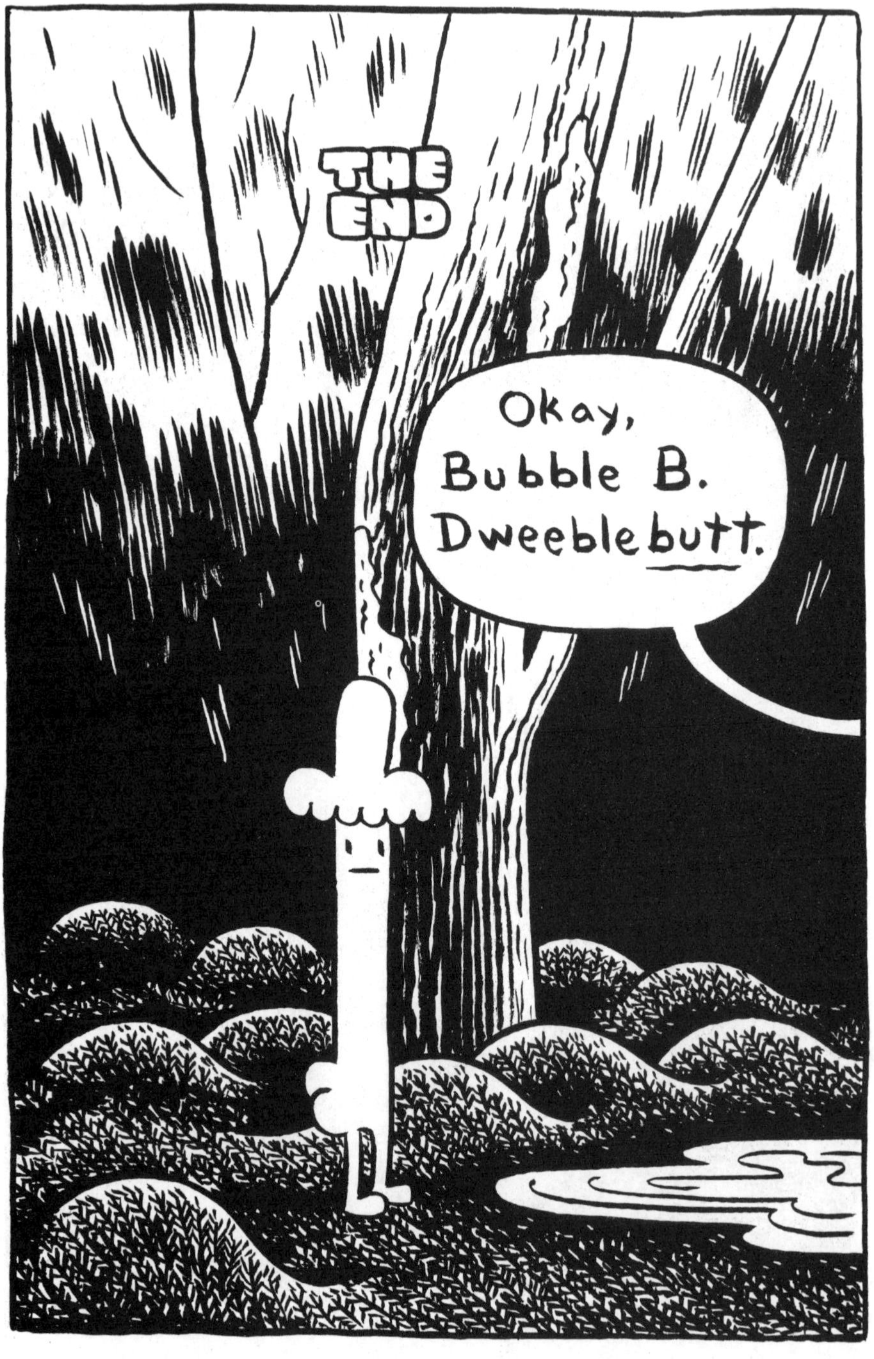
THE END
Okay, Bubble B. Dweeblebutt.

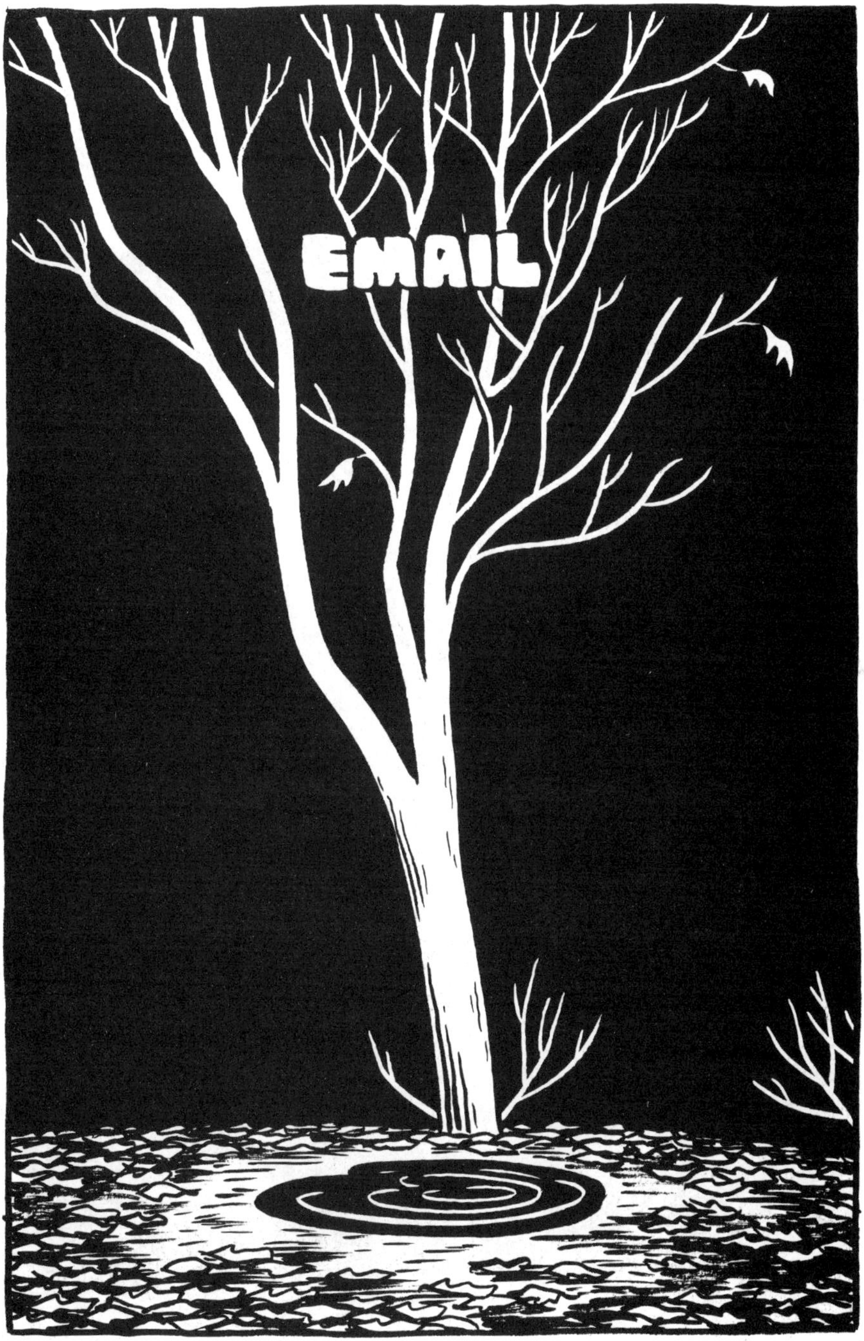
EMAIL

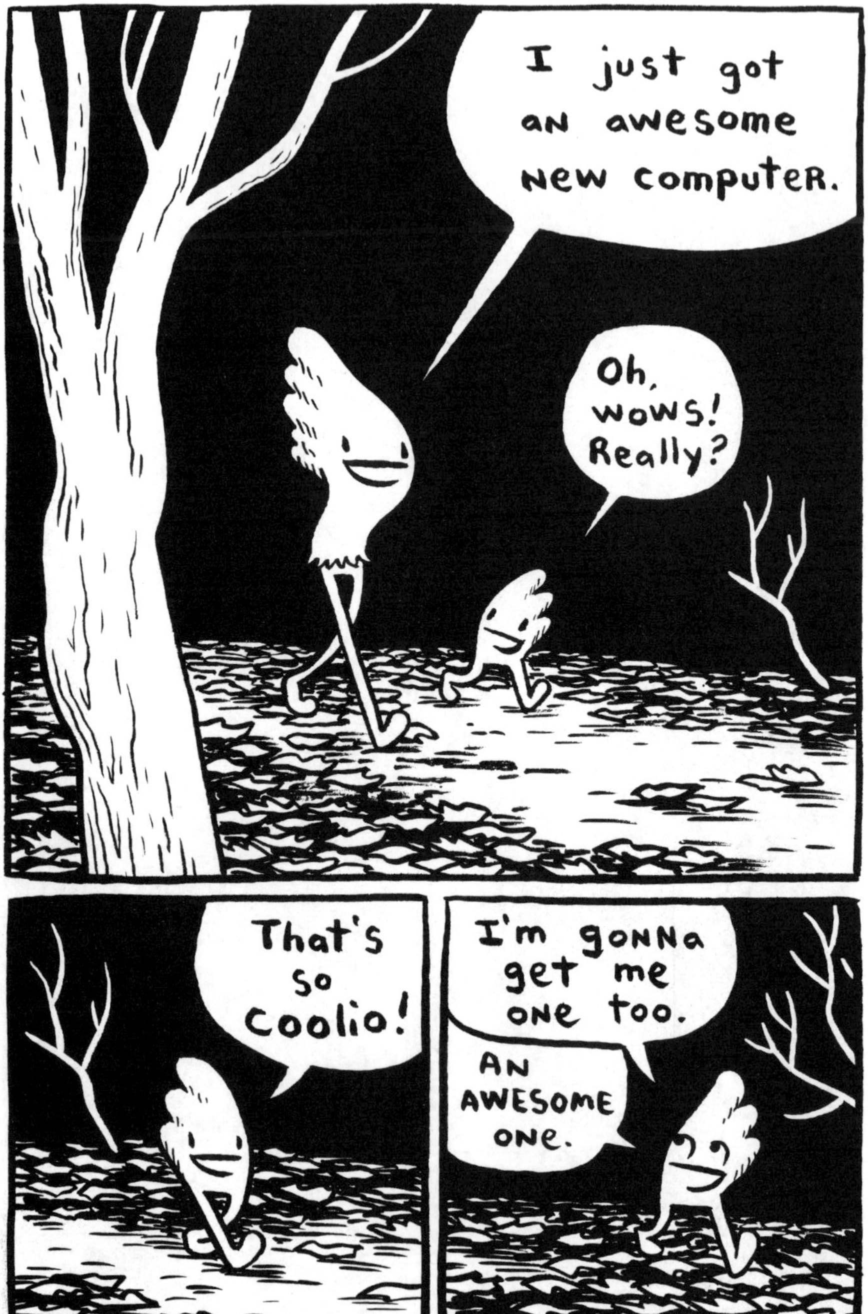
I just got an awesome new computer.
Oh, wows! Really?
That's so coolio!
I'm gonna get me one too.
An awesome one.

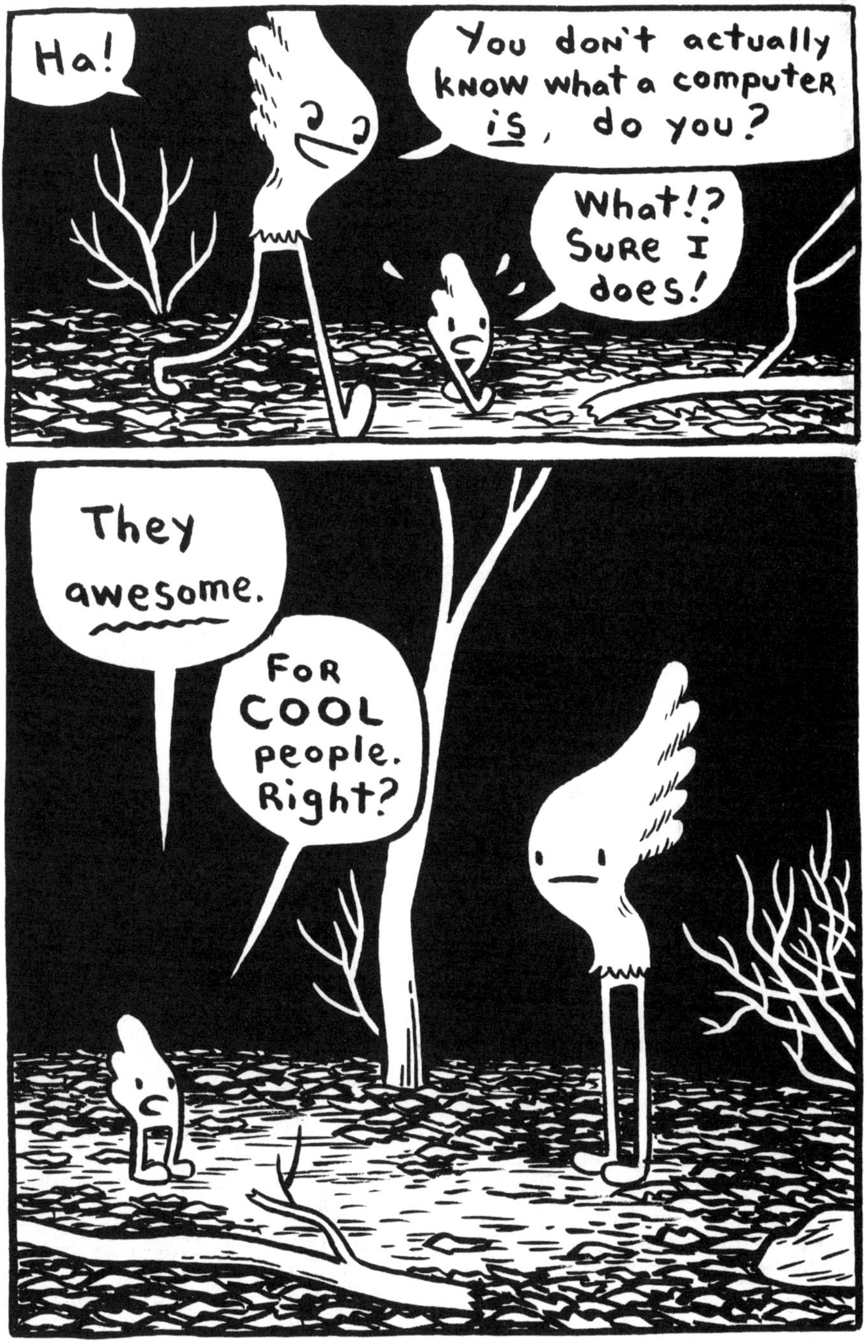
Ha!
You don't actually know what a computer is, do you?
What!? Sure I does!
They awesome.
FOR COOL people. Right?

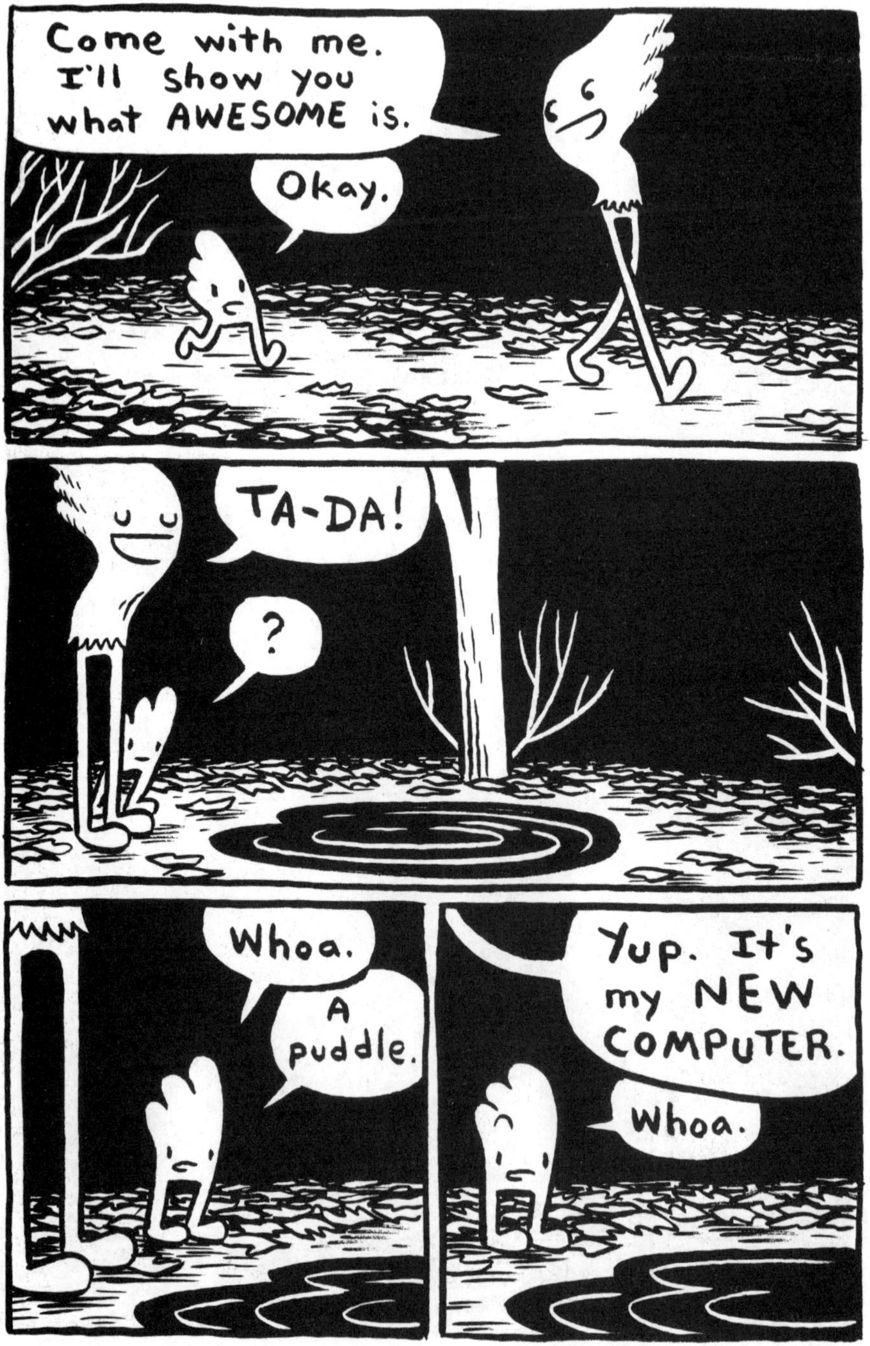
Come with me. I'll show you what AWESOME is.
Okay.
TA-DA!
?
Whoa.
A puddle.
Yup. It's my NEW COMPUTER.
Whoa.

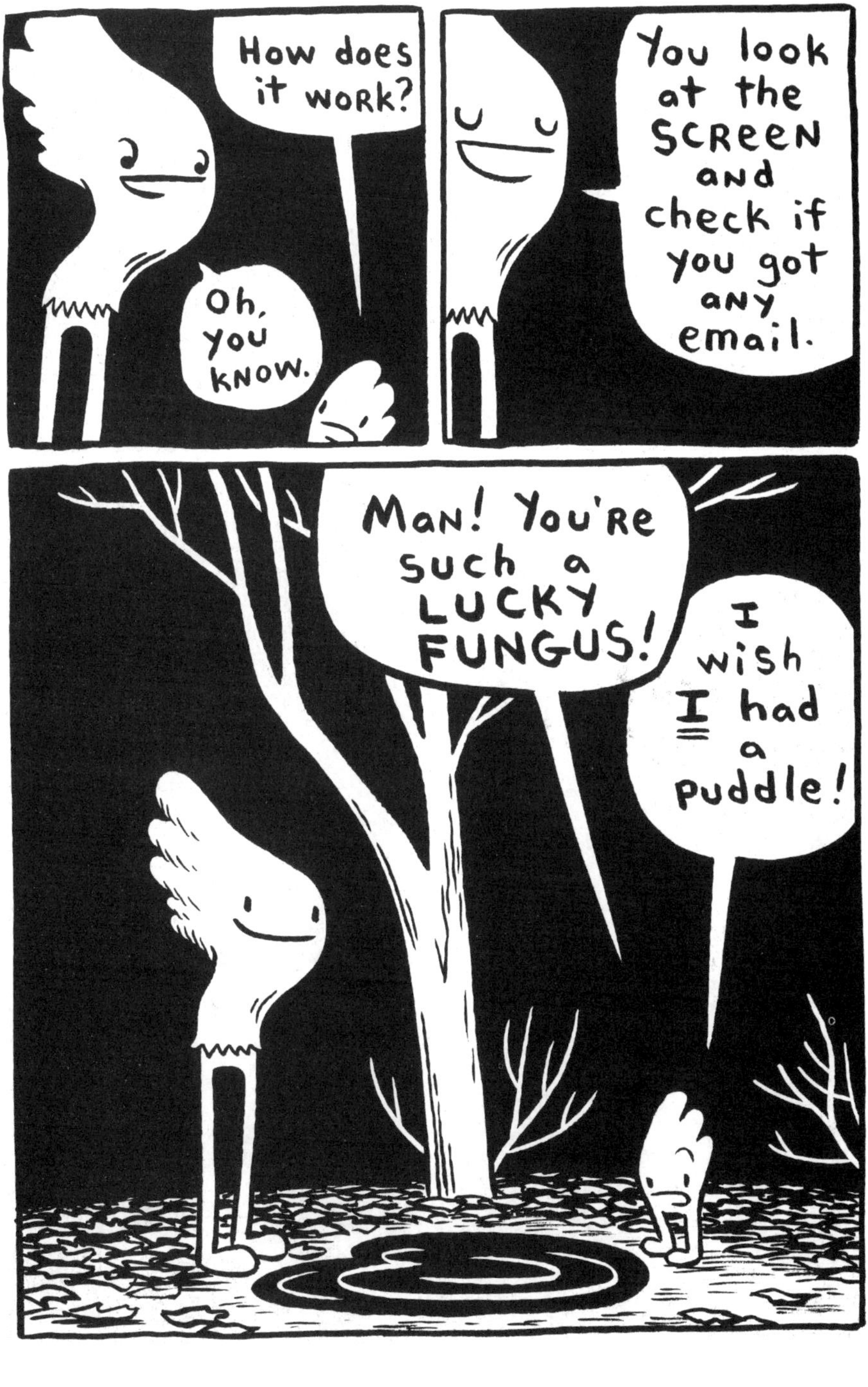
How does it work?
Oh, you know.
You look at the SCREEN and check if you got any email.
Man! You're such a LUCKY FUNGUS!
I wish I had a puddle!

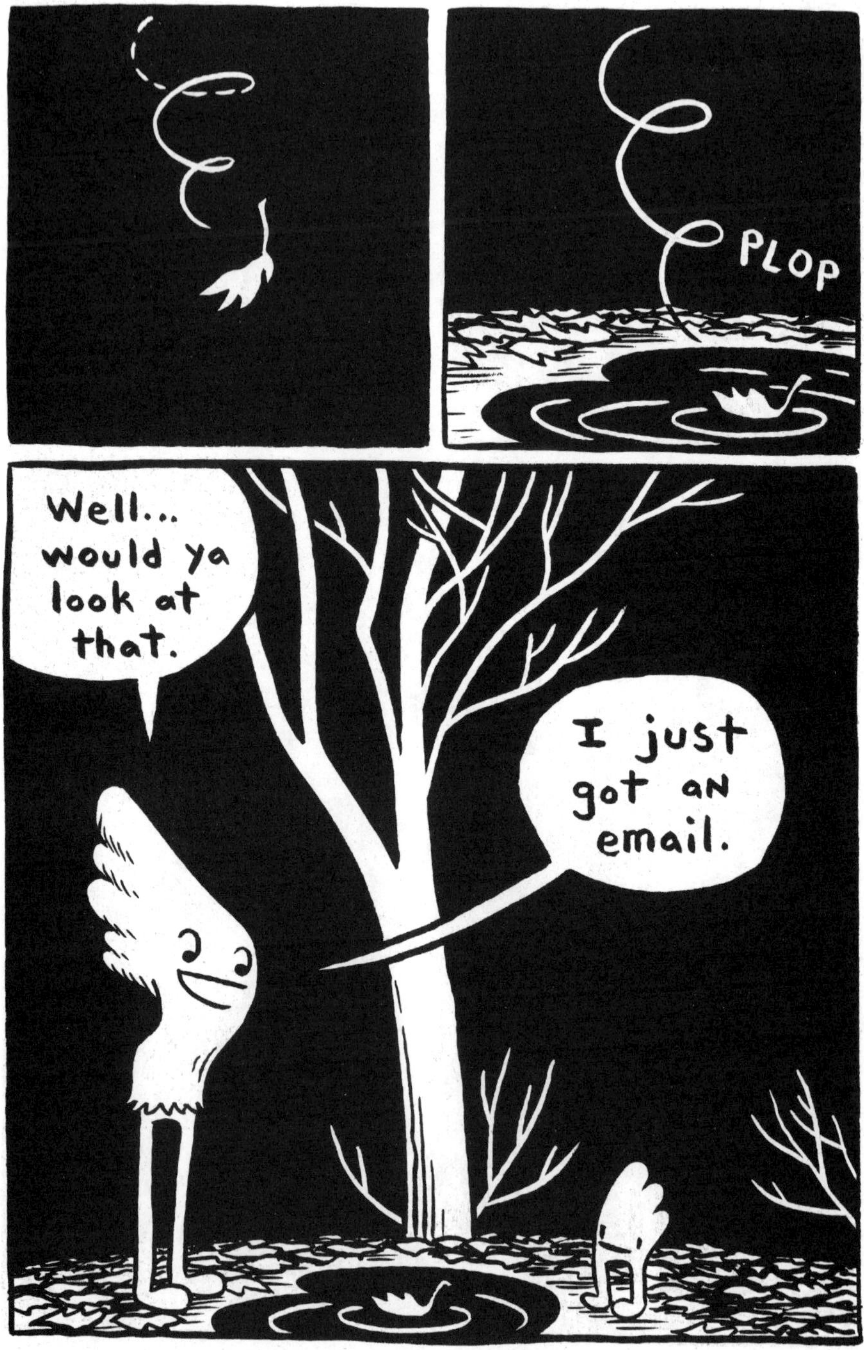
PLOP
Well... would ya look at that.
I just got an email.

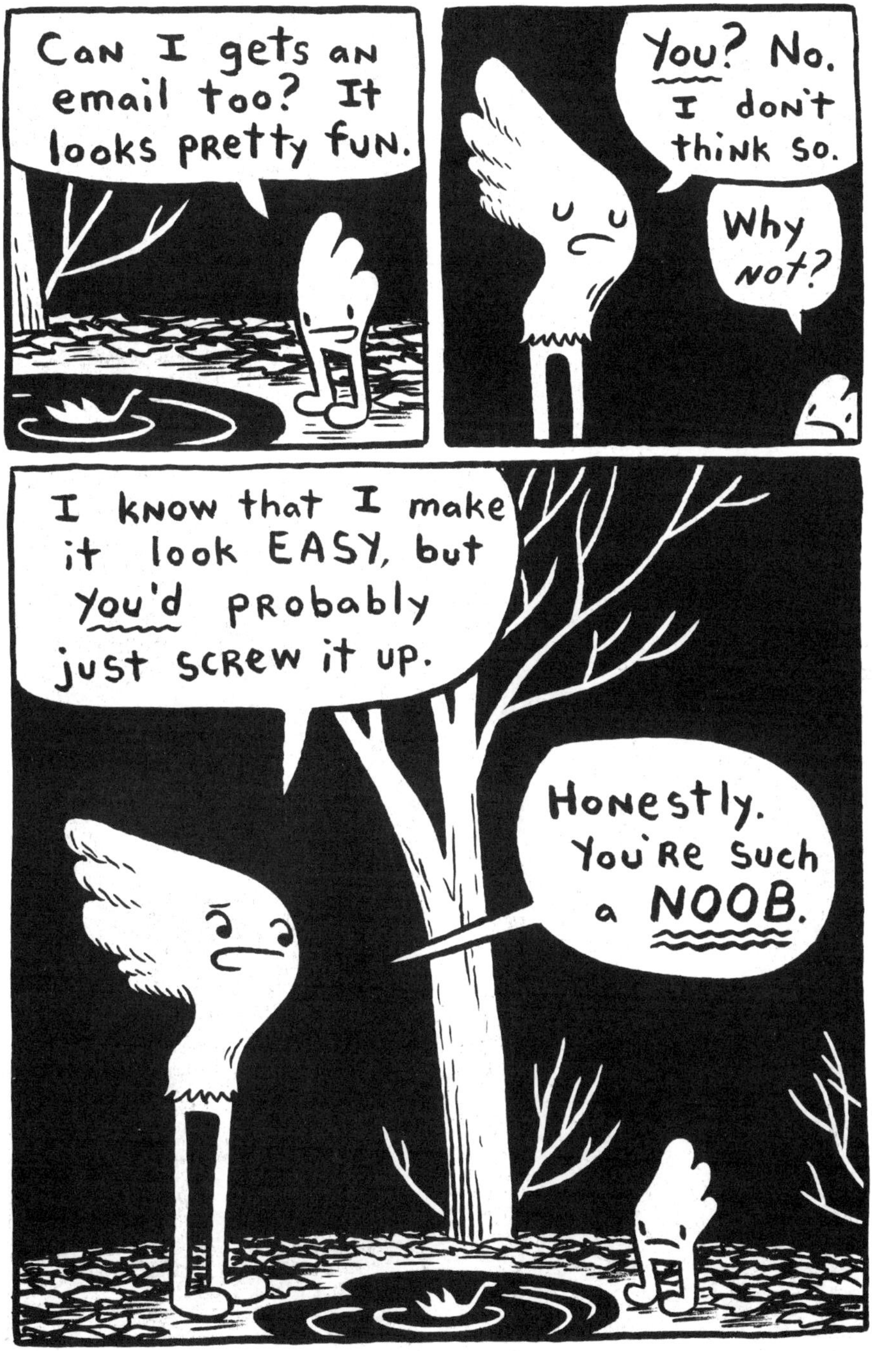
Can I gets an email too? It looks pretty fun.
You? No. I don't think so.
Why not?
I know that I make it look EASY, but you'd probably just screw it up.
Honestly. You're such a NOOB.

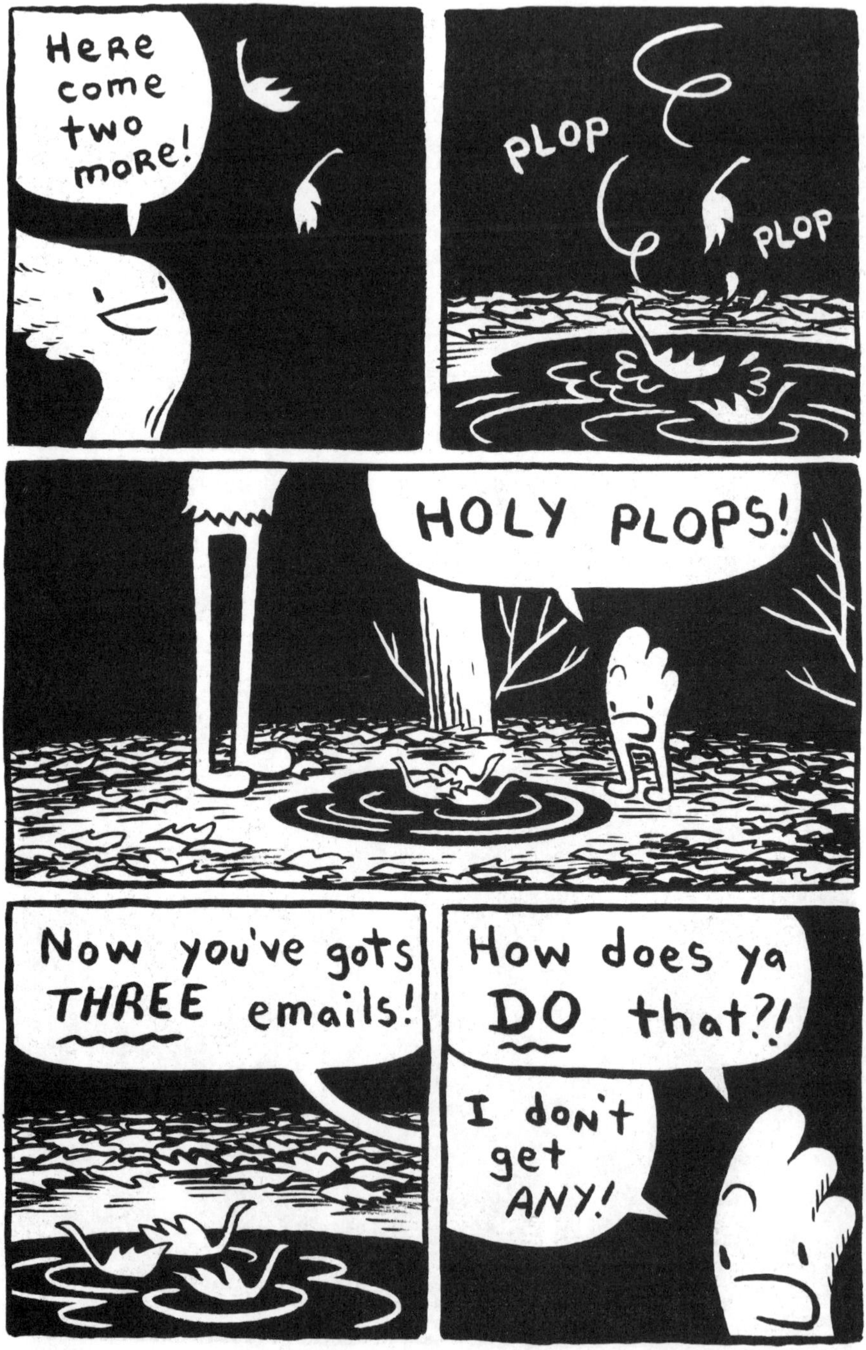
Here come two more!
PLOP
PLOP
HOLY PLOPS!
Now you've gots THREE emails!
How does ya DO that?!
I don't get ANY!

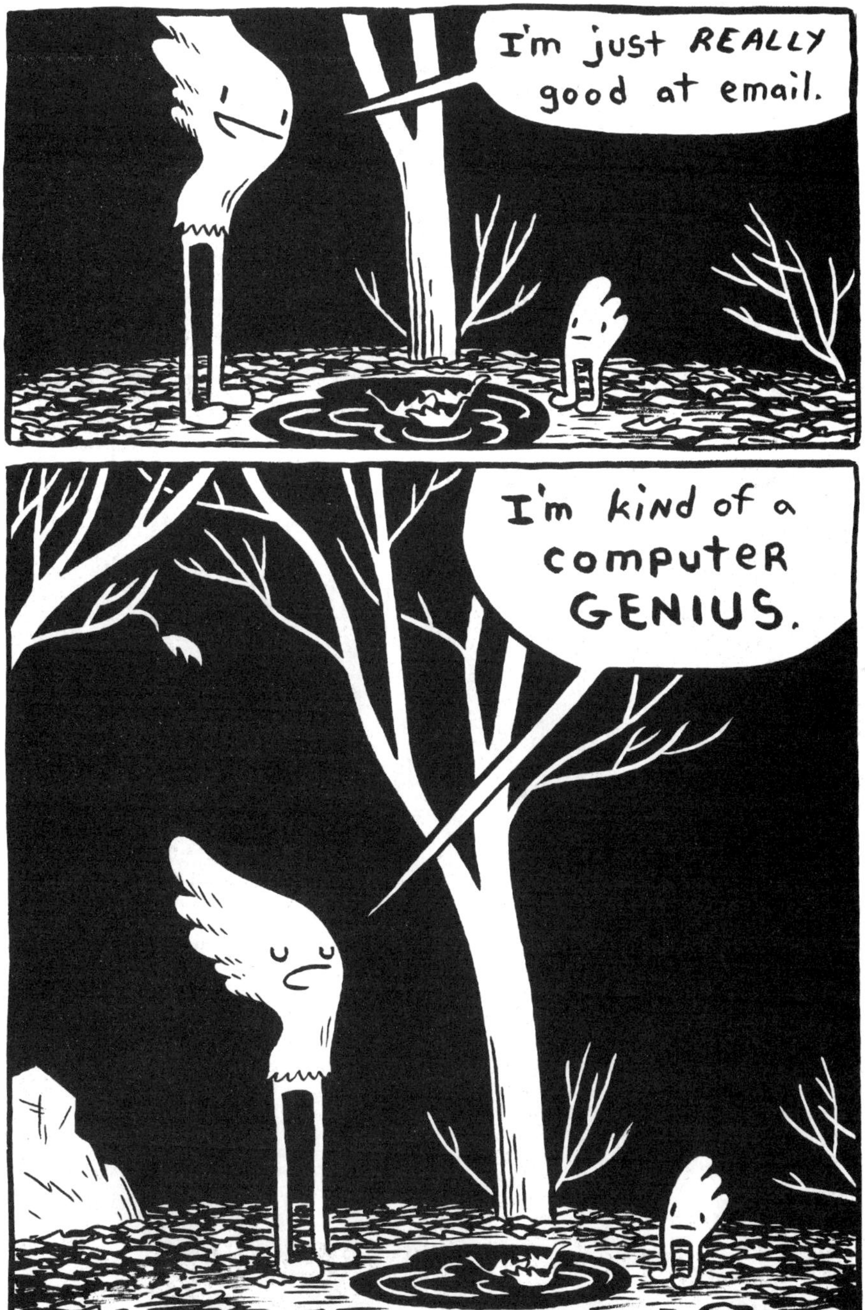
I'm just REALLY good at email.
I'm kind of a computer GENIUS.

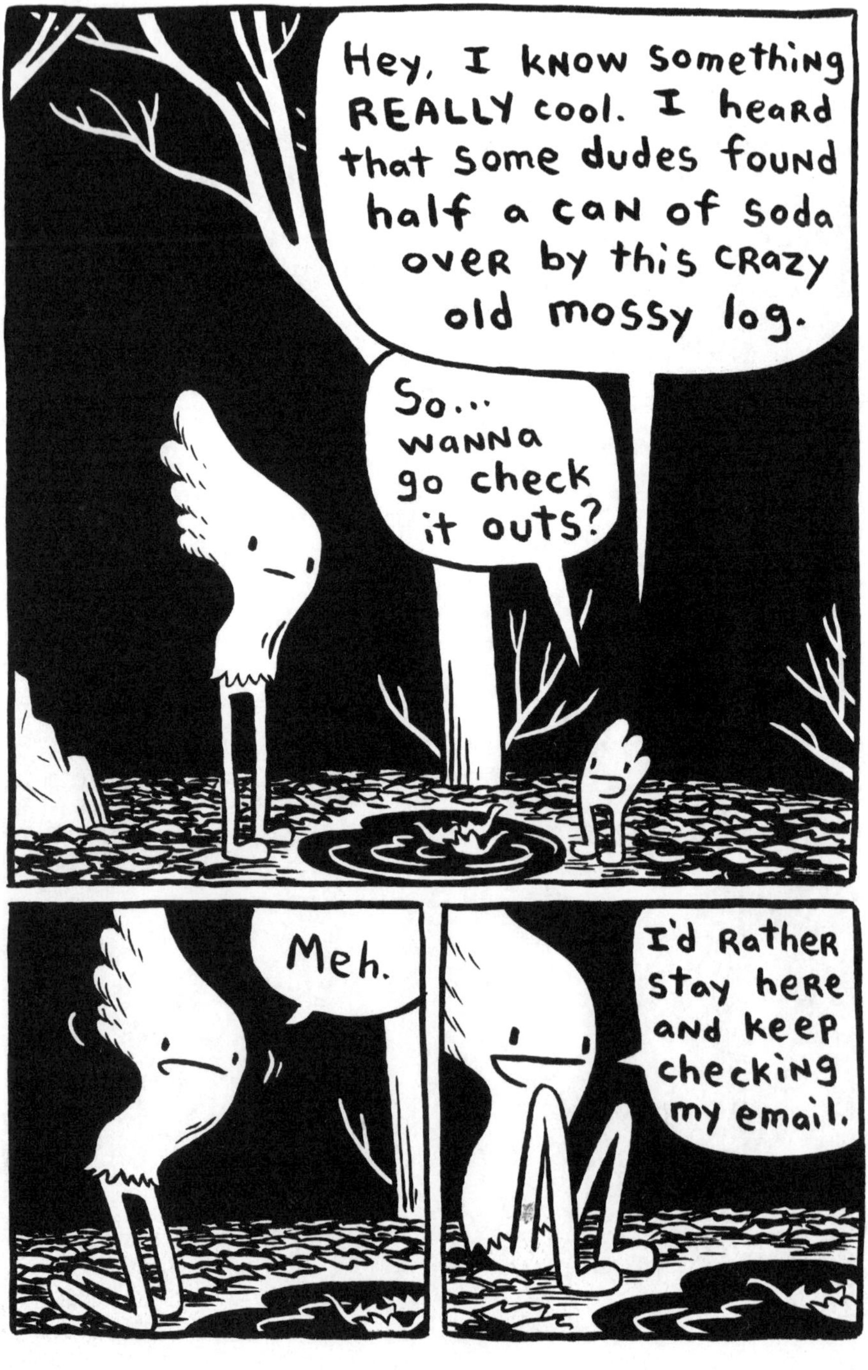
Hey, I know something REALLY cool. I heard that some dudes found half a can of soda over by this crazy old mossy log.
So... wanna go check it outs?
Meh.
I'd rather stay here and keep checking my email.

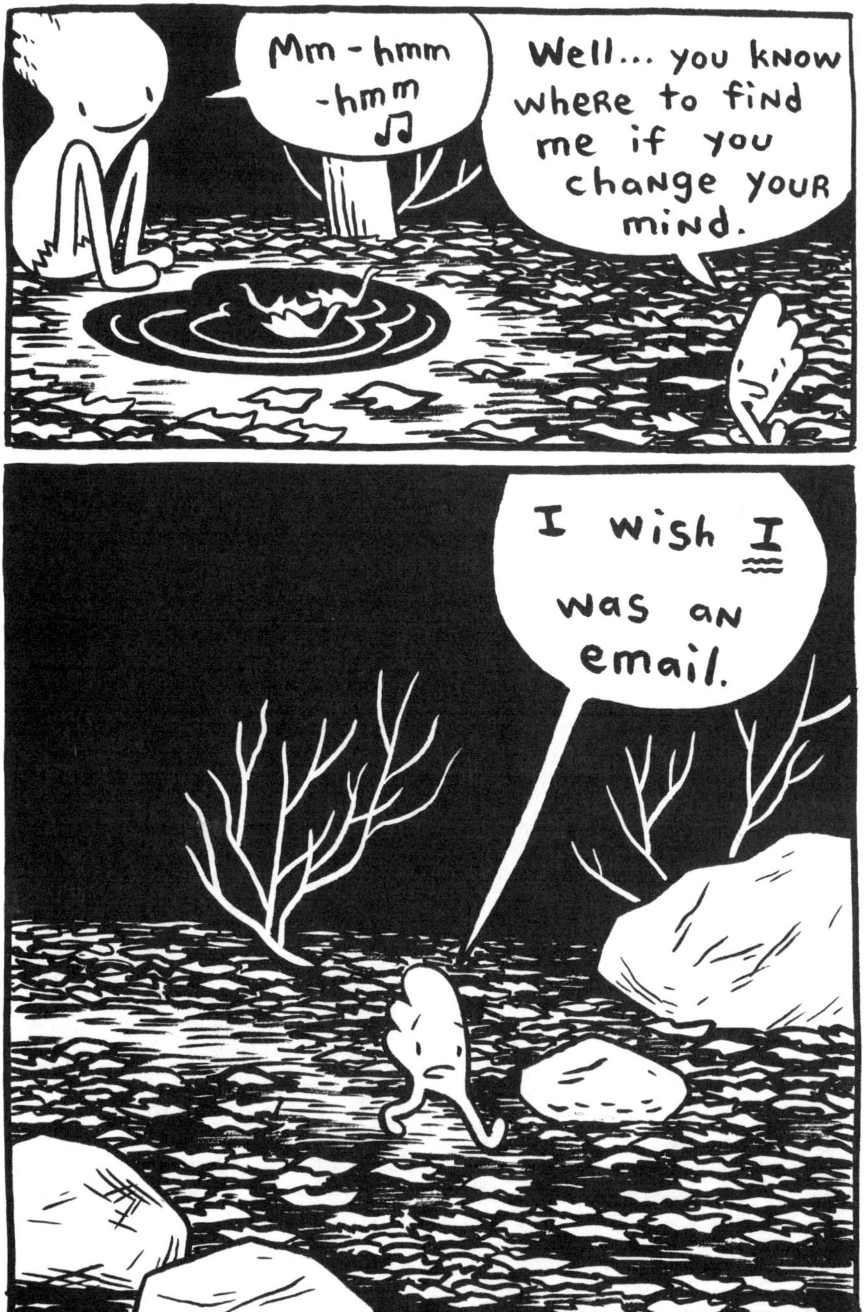
Mm-hmm -hmm ♫
Well... you know where to find me if you change your mind.
I wish I was an email.

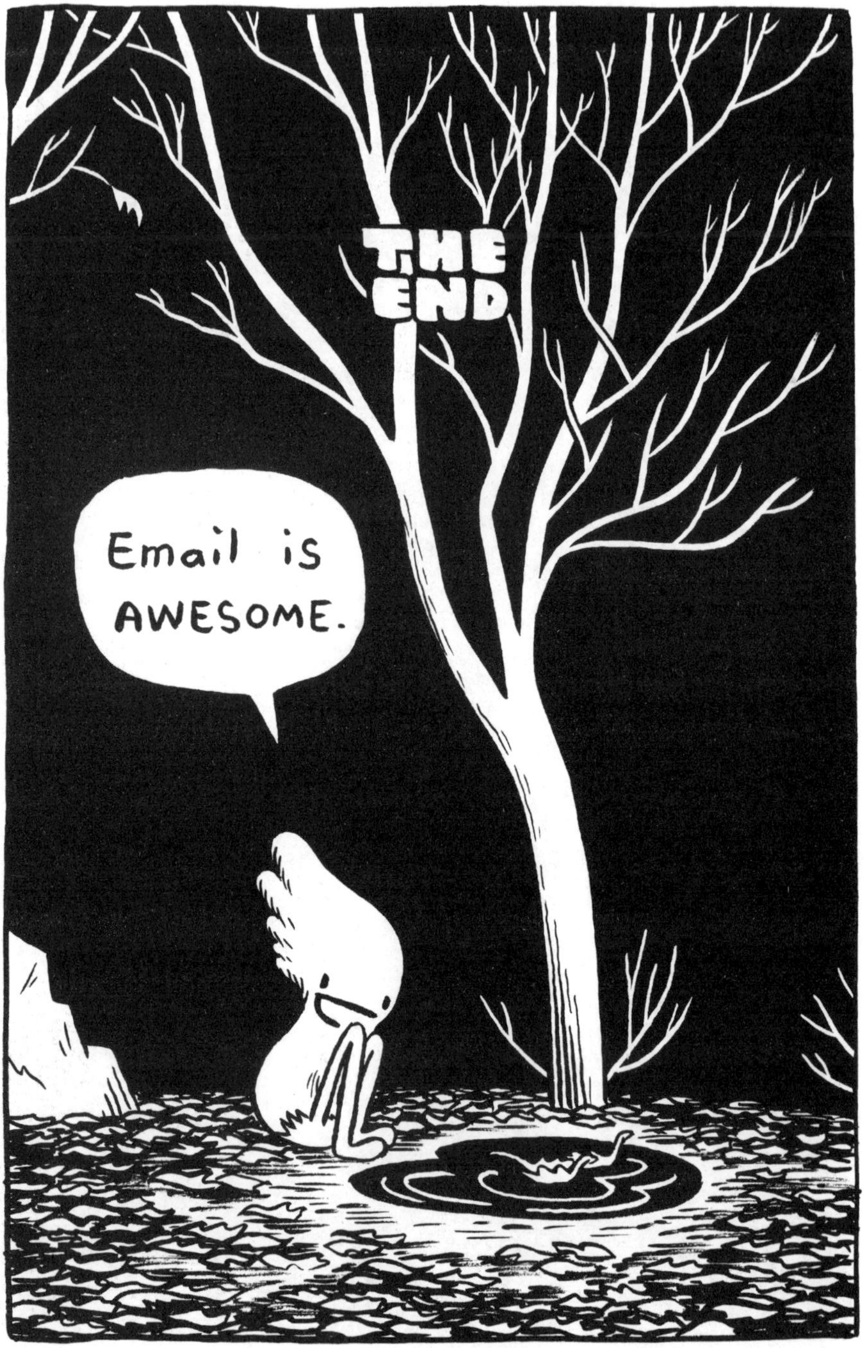
THE END
Email is AWESOME.

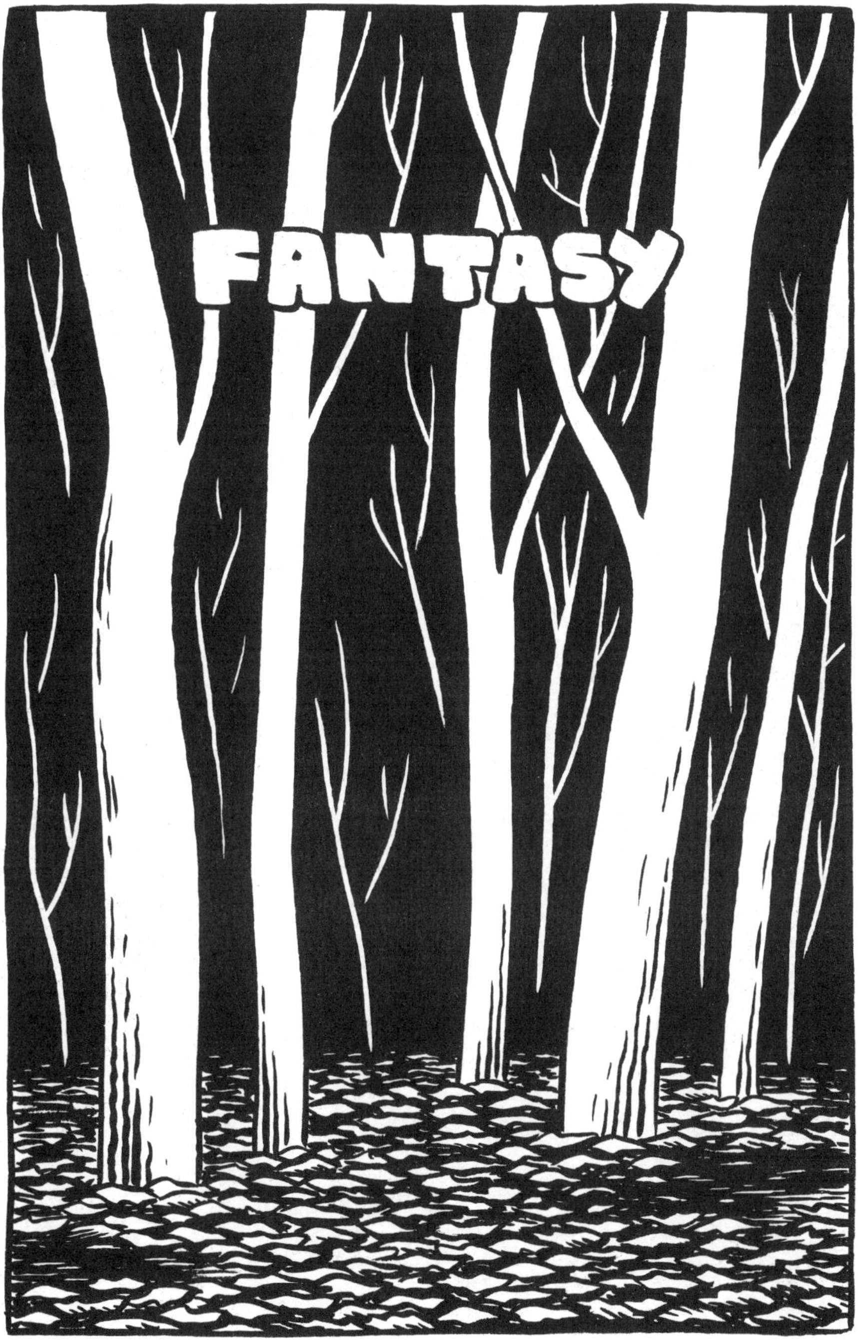
FANTASY

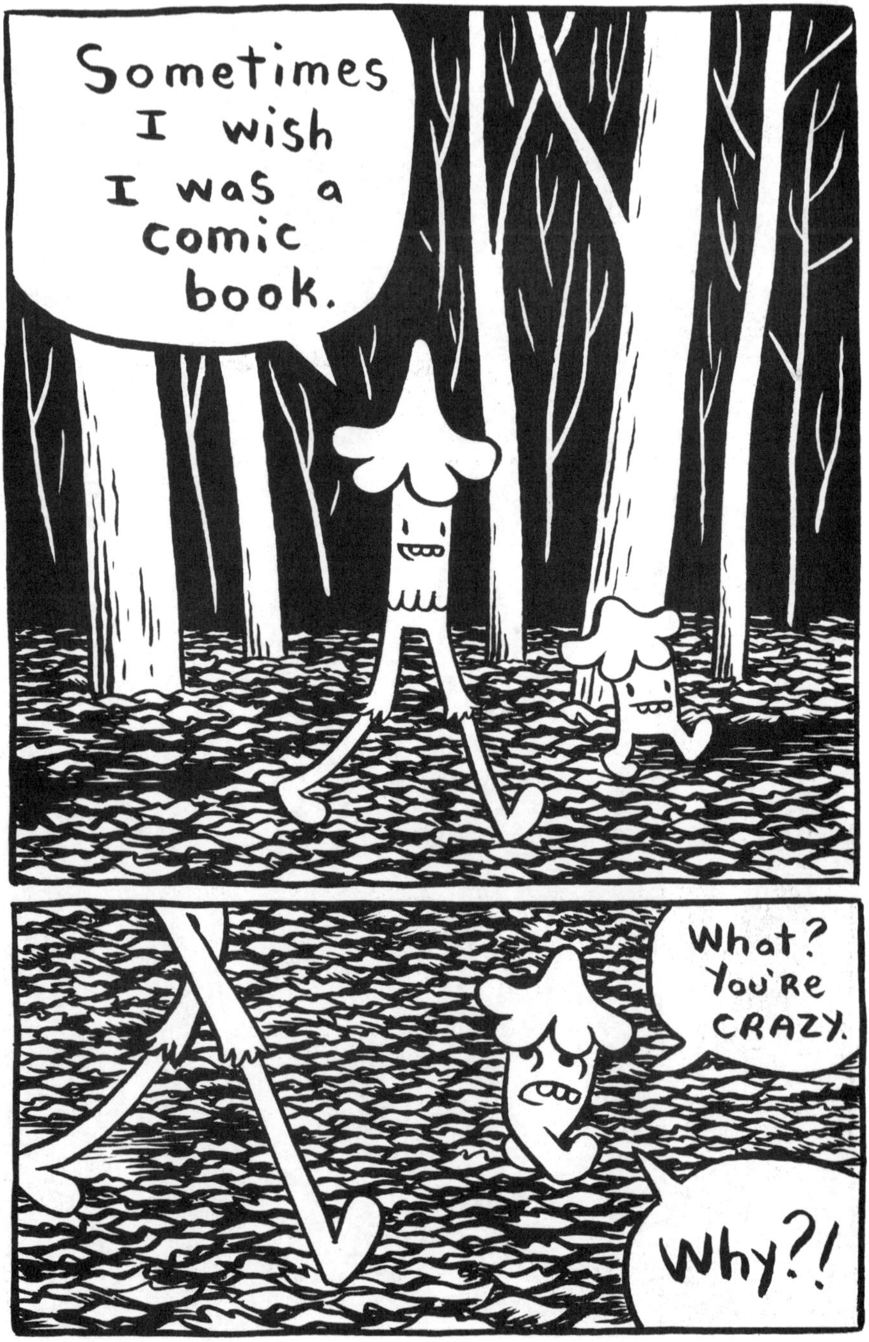
Sometimes I wish I was a comic book.
What? You're CRAZY.
Why?!

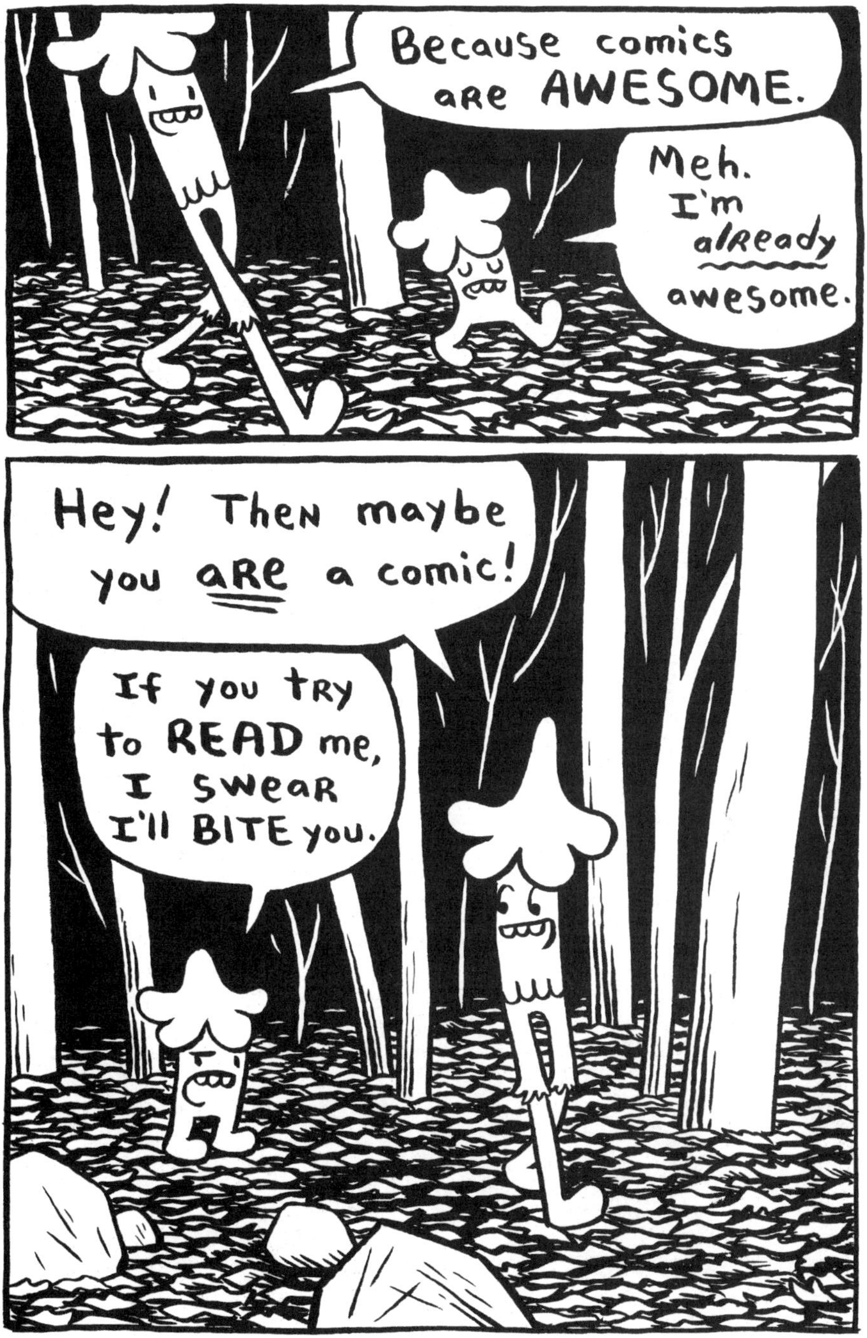
Because comics are AWESOME.
Meh. I'm already awesome.
Hey! Then maybe you ARE a comic!
If you try to READ me, I swear I'll BITE you.

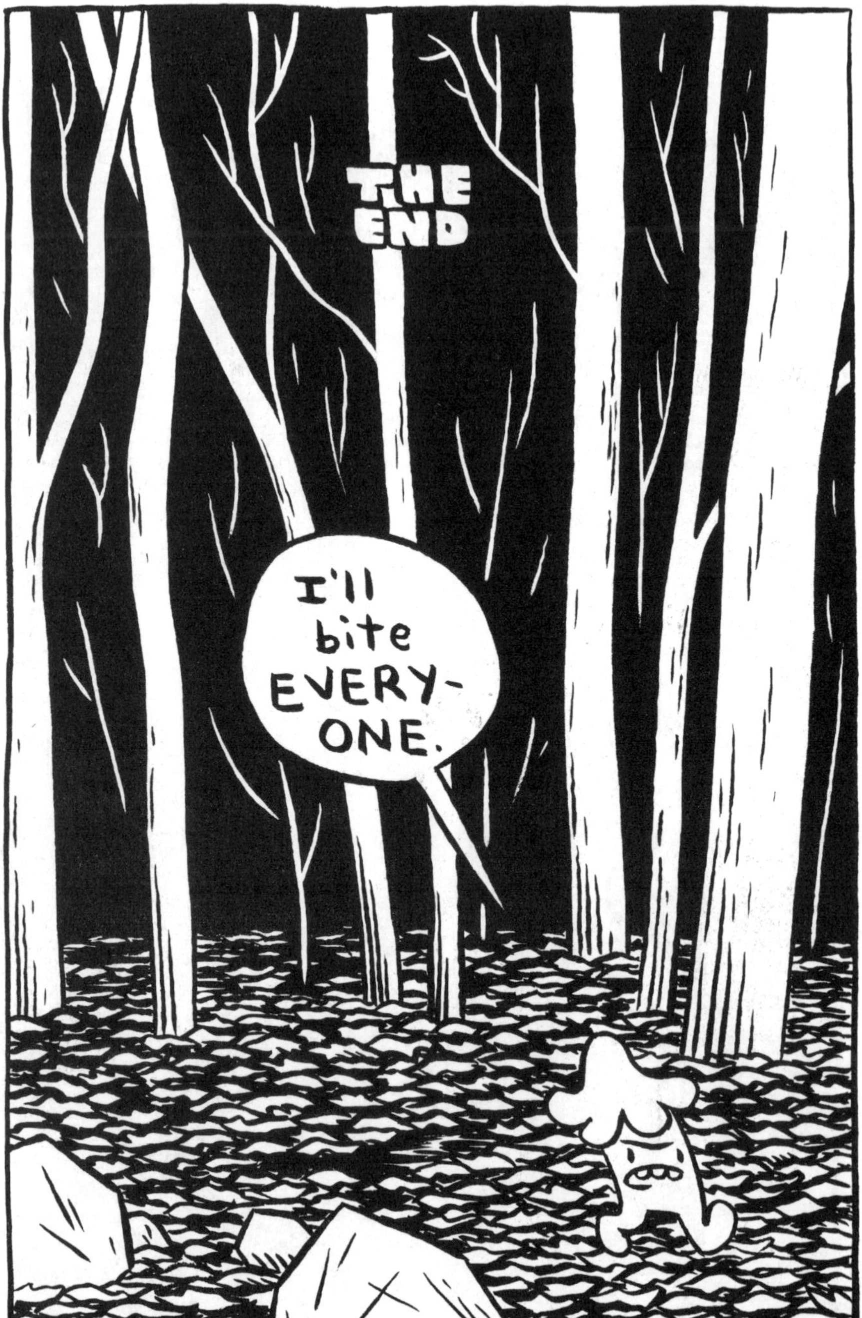
THE END
I'll bite EVERY-ONE.

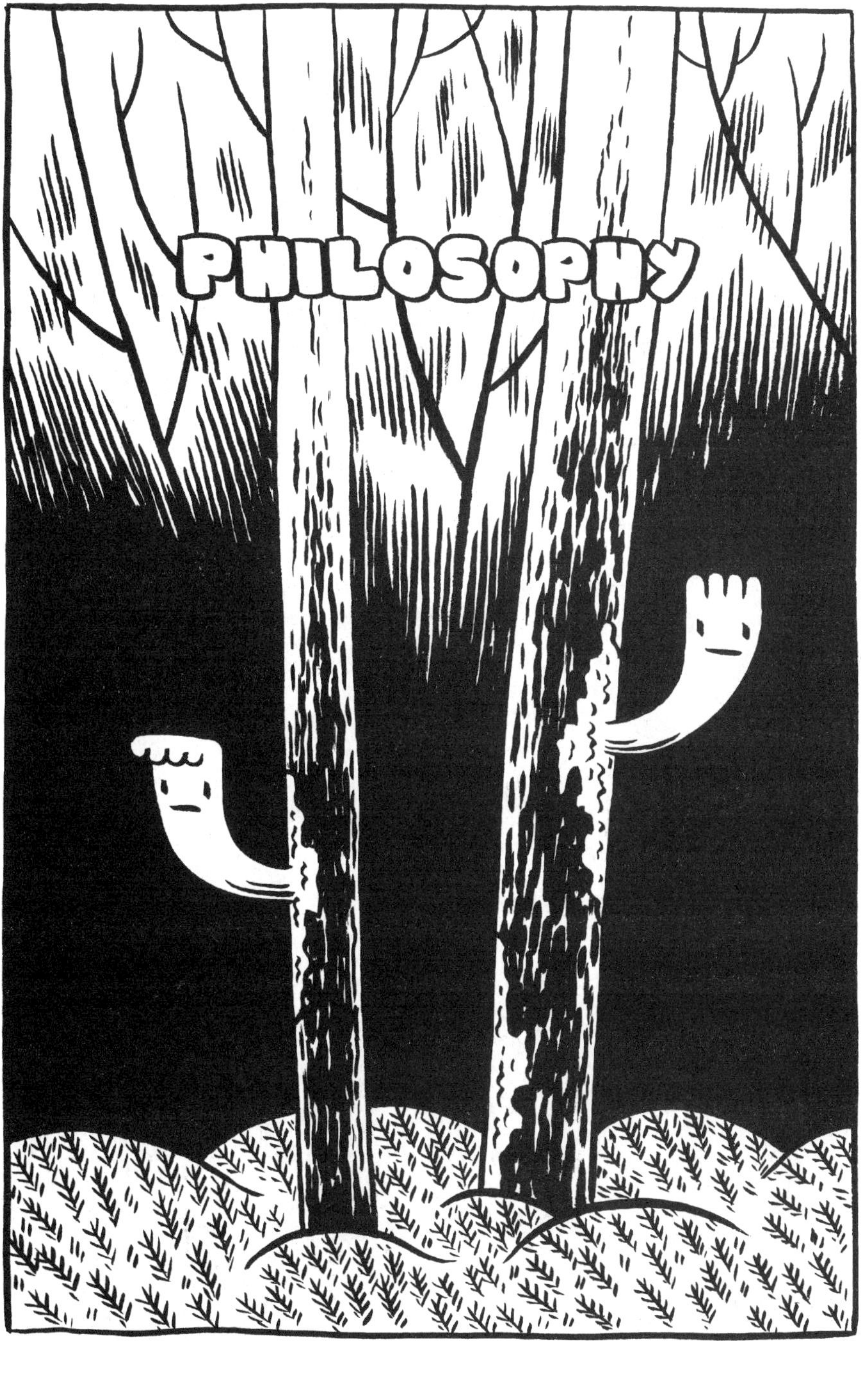
PHILOSOPHY

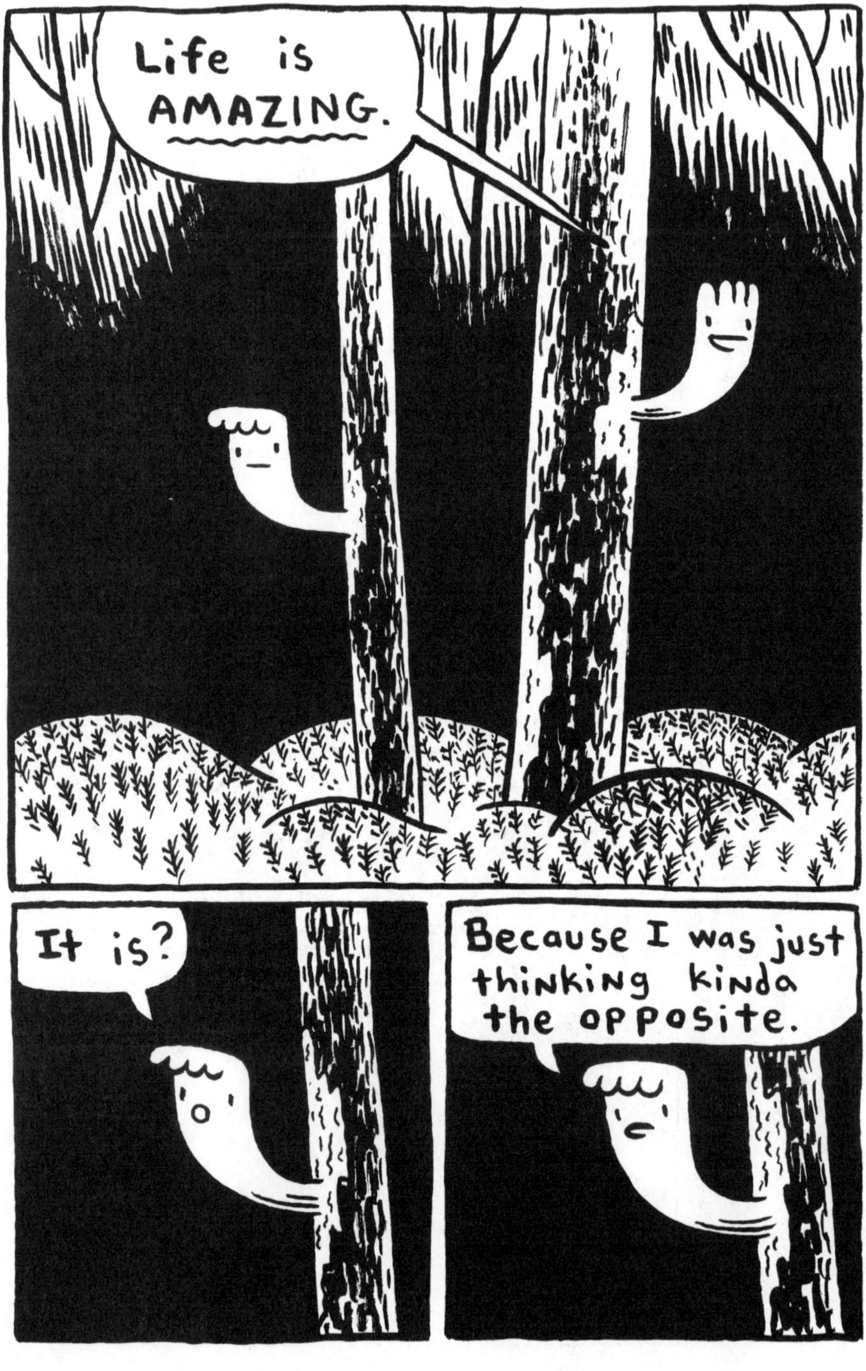
Life is AMAZING.
It is?
Because I was just thinking kinda the opposite.

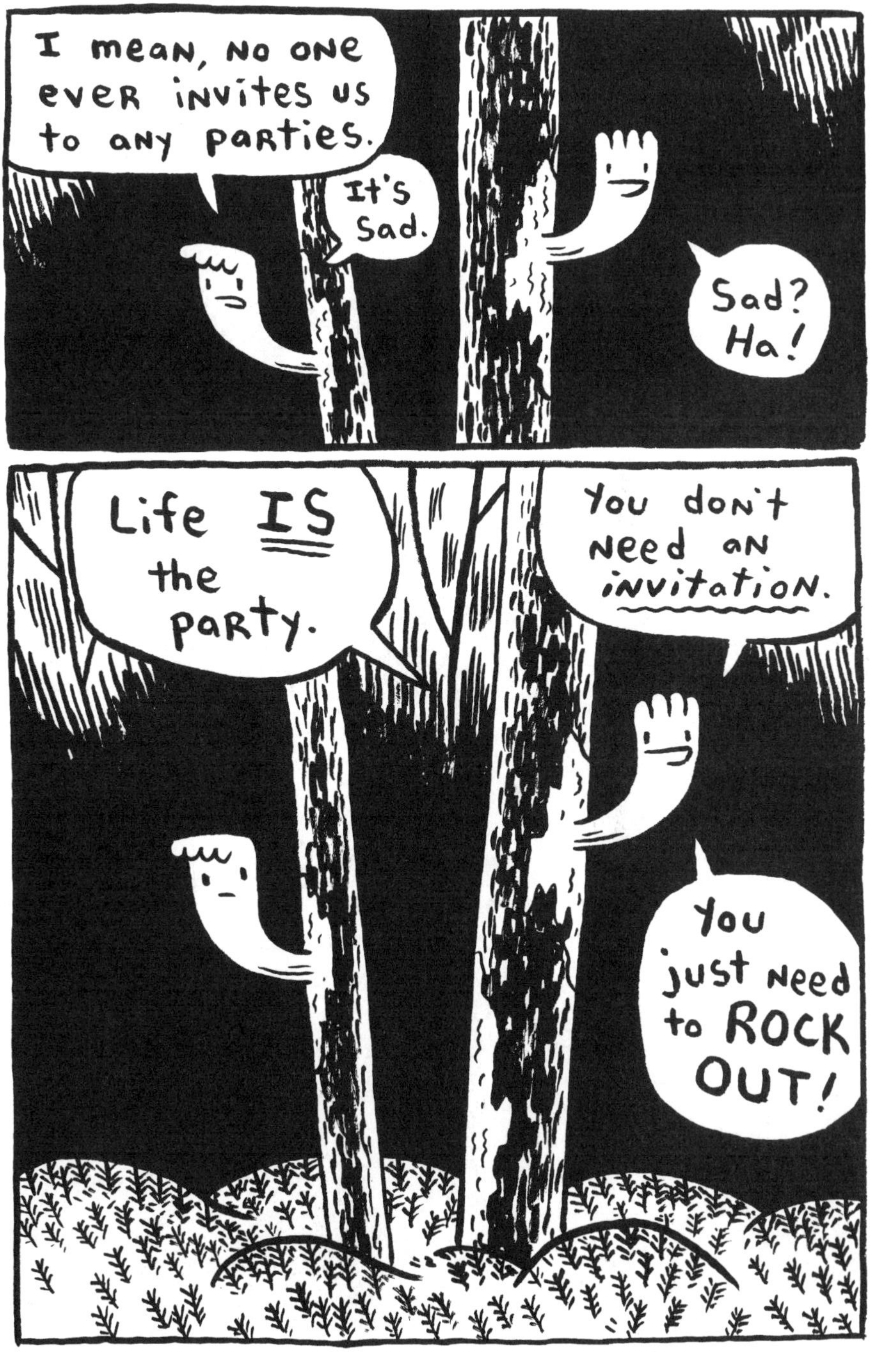
I mean, no one ever invites us to any parties.
It's Sad.
Sad? Ha!
Life IS the party.
You don't need an invitation.
You just need to ROCK OUT!

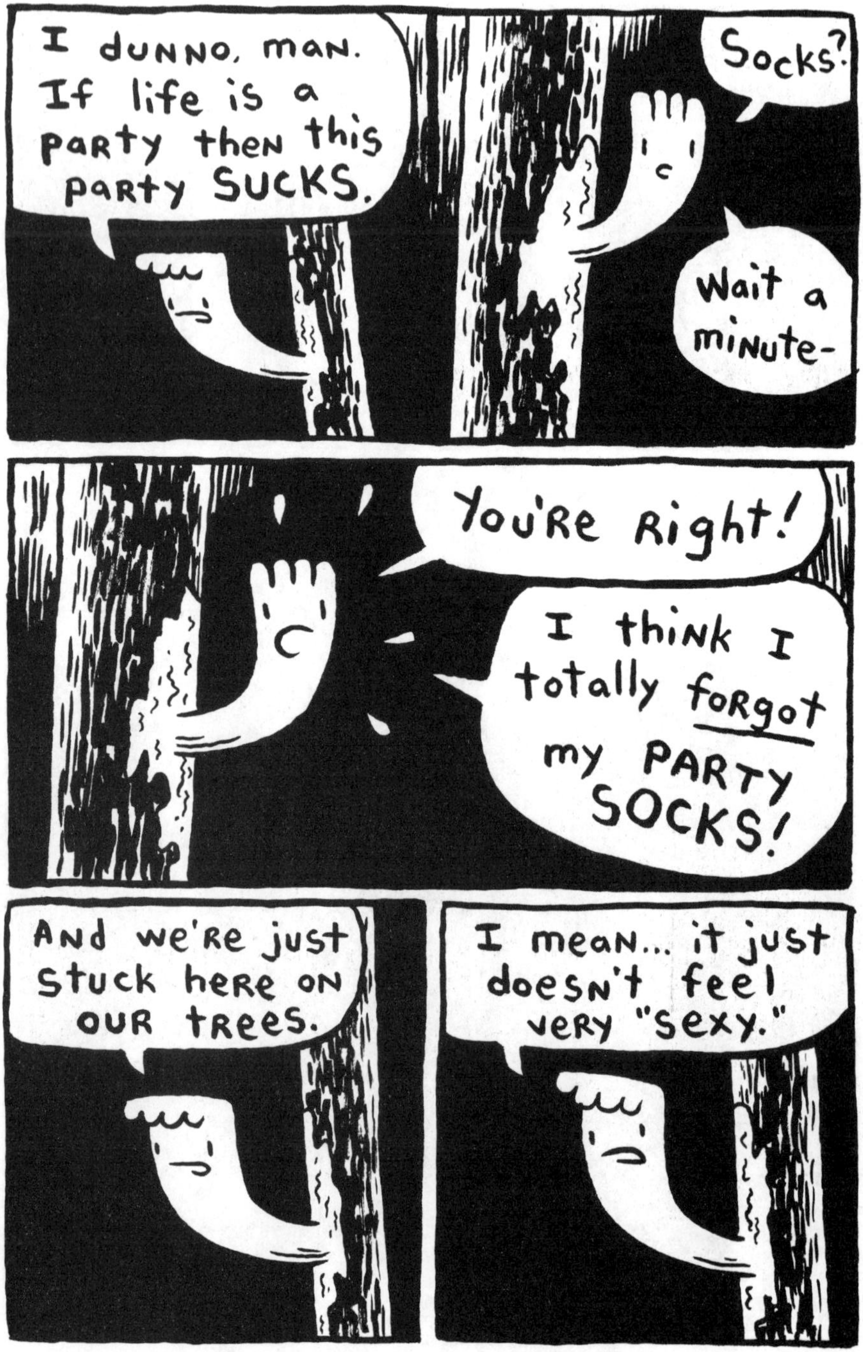
I dunno, man. If life is a party then this party SUCKS.
Socks?
Wait a minute-
You're Right!
I think I totally forgot my PARTY SOCKS!
And we're just stuck here on our trees.
I mean... it just doesn't feel very "sexy."

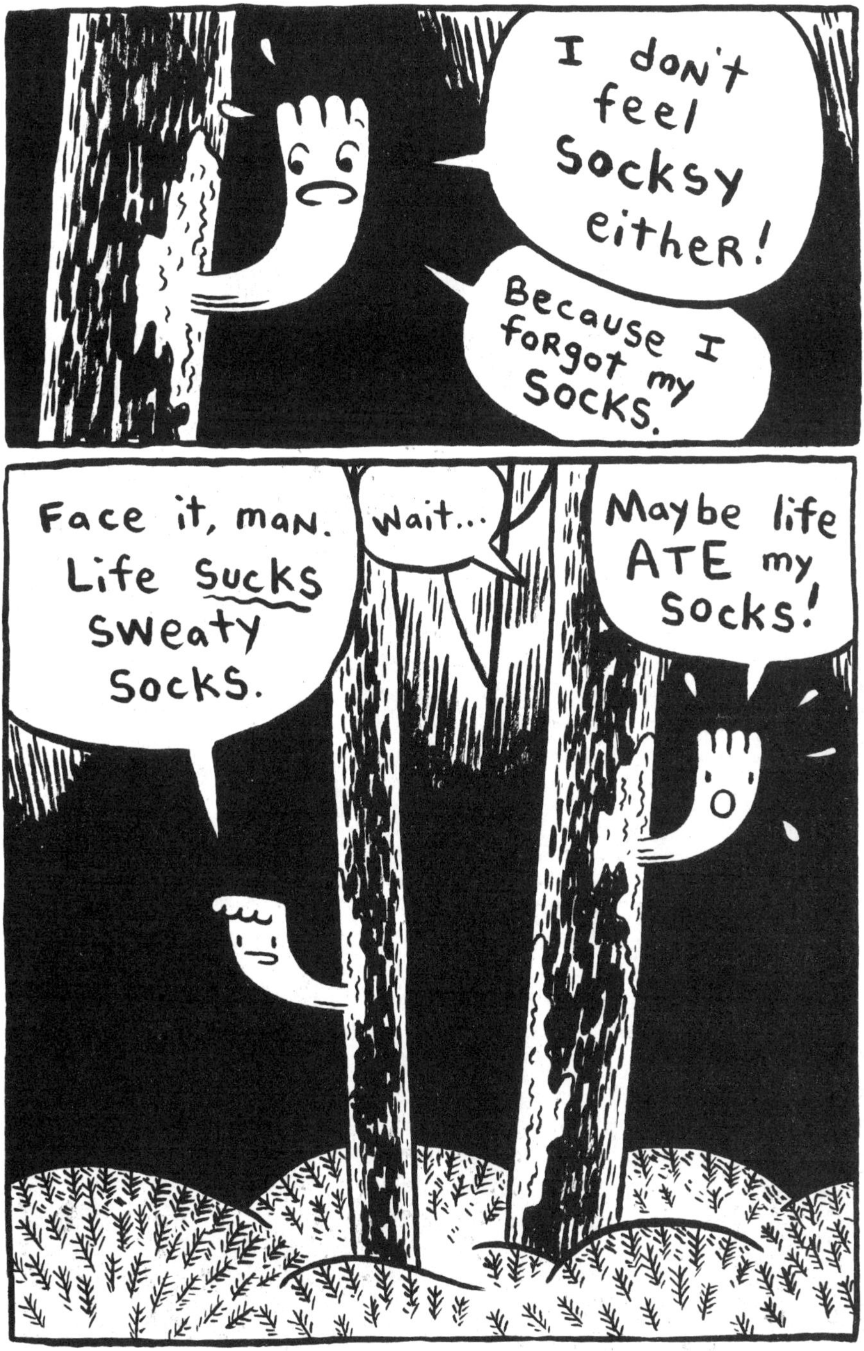
I don't feel socksy either!
Because I forgot my socks.
Face it, man. Life sucks sweaty socks.
Wait...
Maybe life ATE my socks!

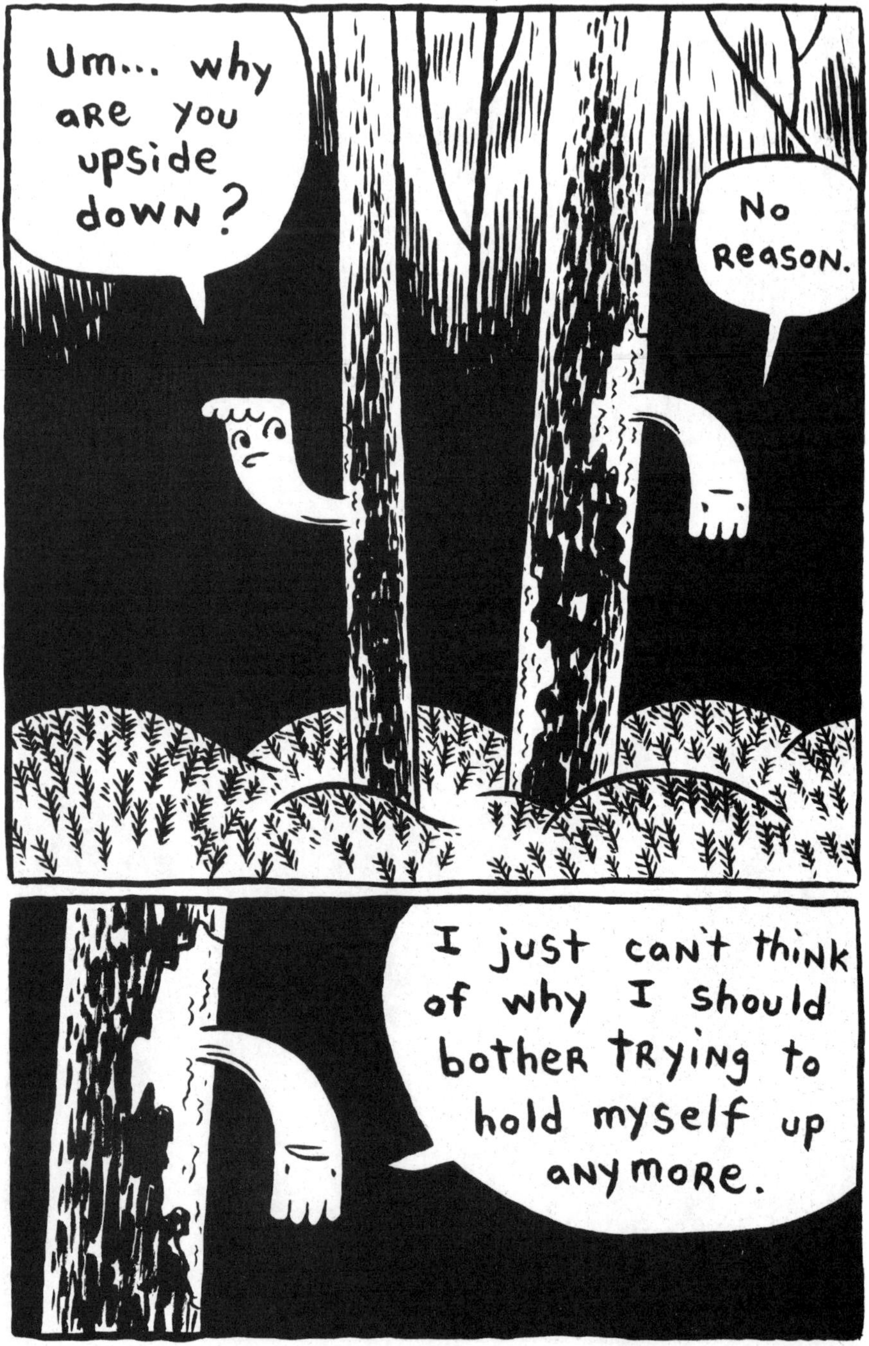
Um... why are you upside down?
No reason.
I just can't think of why I should bother trying to hold myself up anymore.

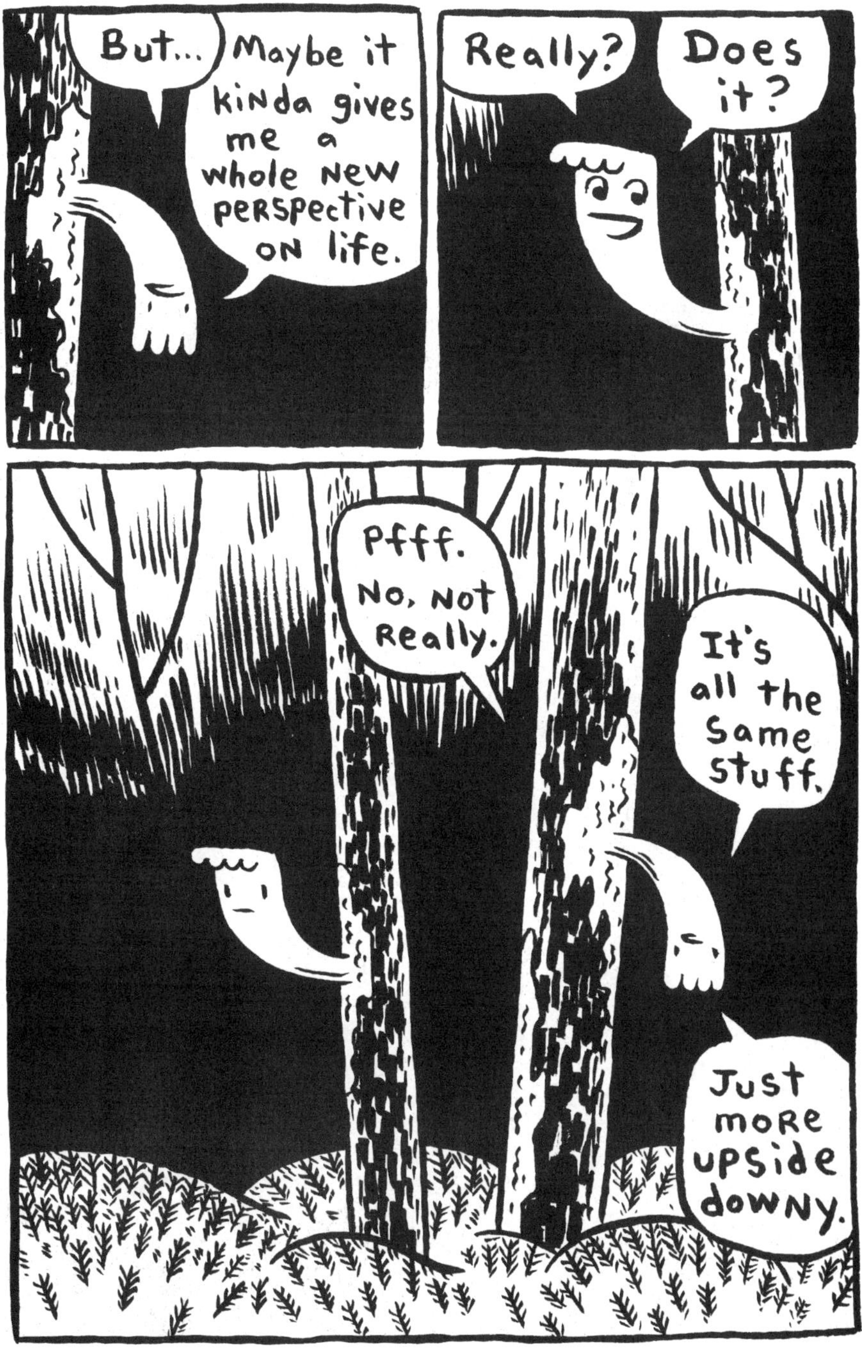
But...
Maybe it kinda gives me a whole new perspective on life.
Really?
Does it?
Pfff. No, not really.
It's all the same stuff.
Just more upside downy.

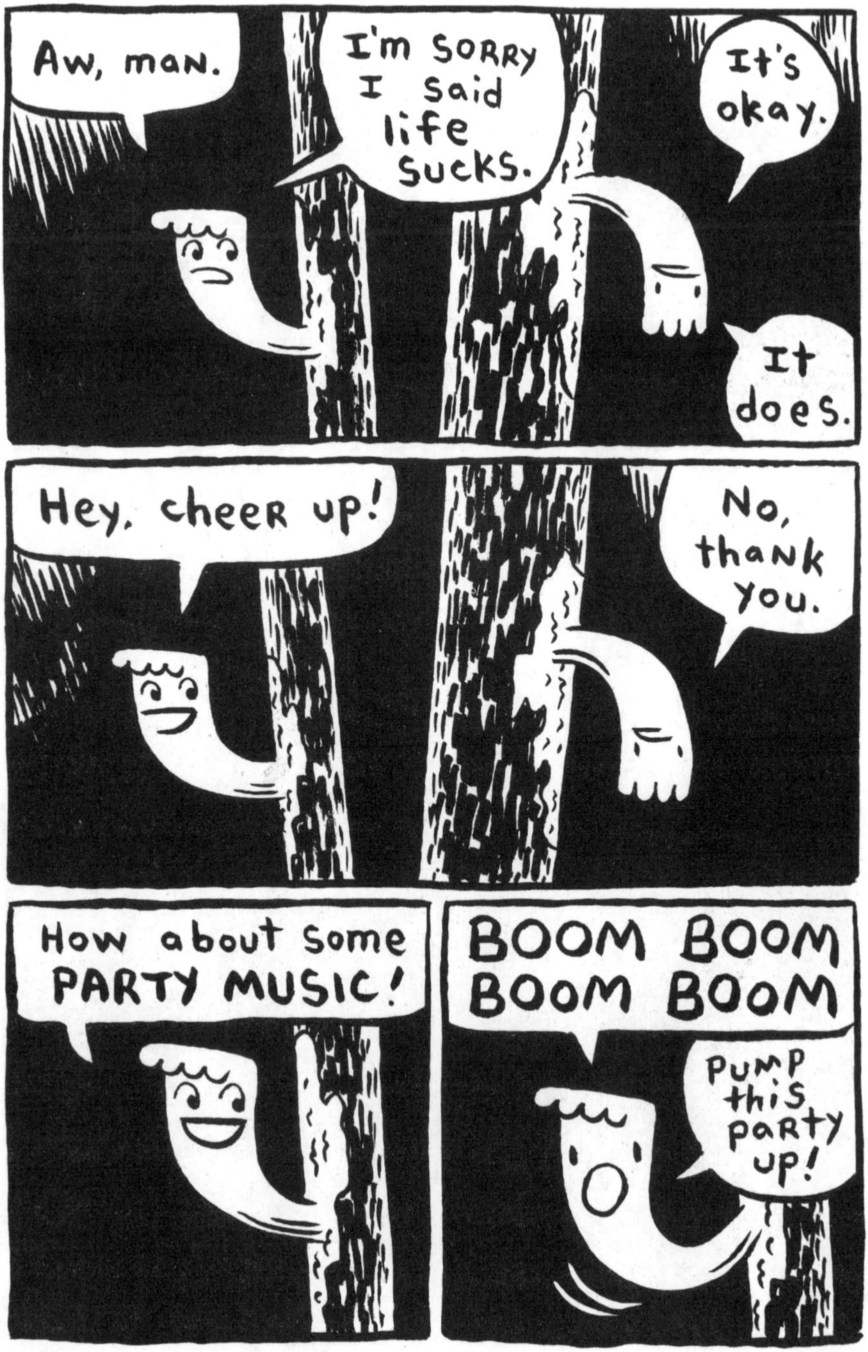
Aw, man.
I'm SORRY I said life sucks.
It's okay.
It does.
Hey, cheer up!
No, thank you.
How about some PARTY MUSIC!
BOOM BOOM BOOM BOOM
Pump this party up!

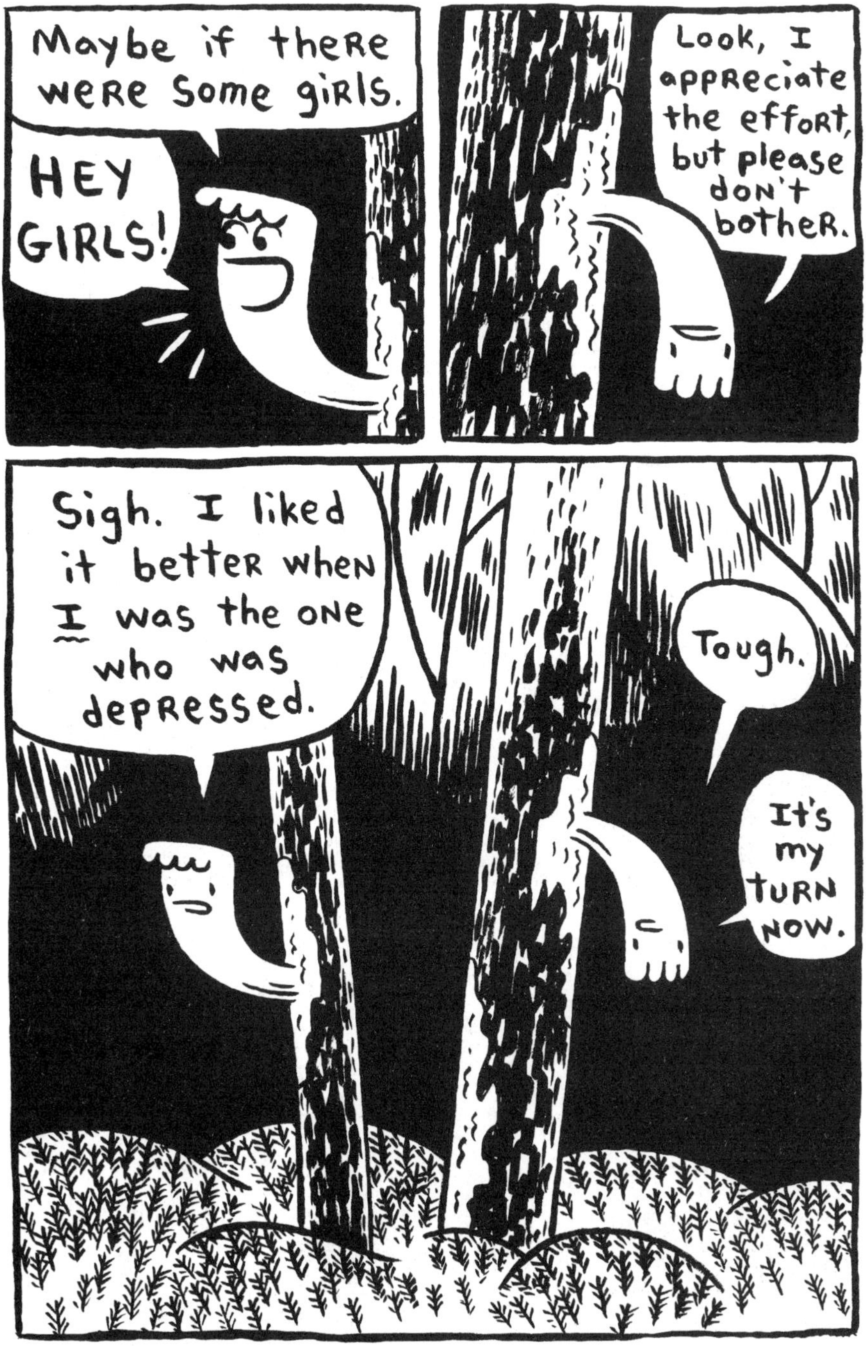
Maybe if there were some girls.
HEY GIRLS!
Look, I appreciate the effort, but please don't bother.
Sigh. I liked it better when I was the one who was depressed.
Tough.
It's my TURN NOW.

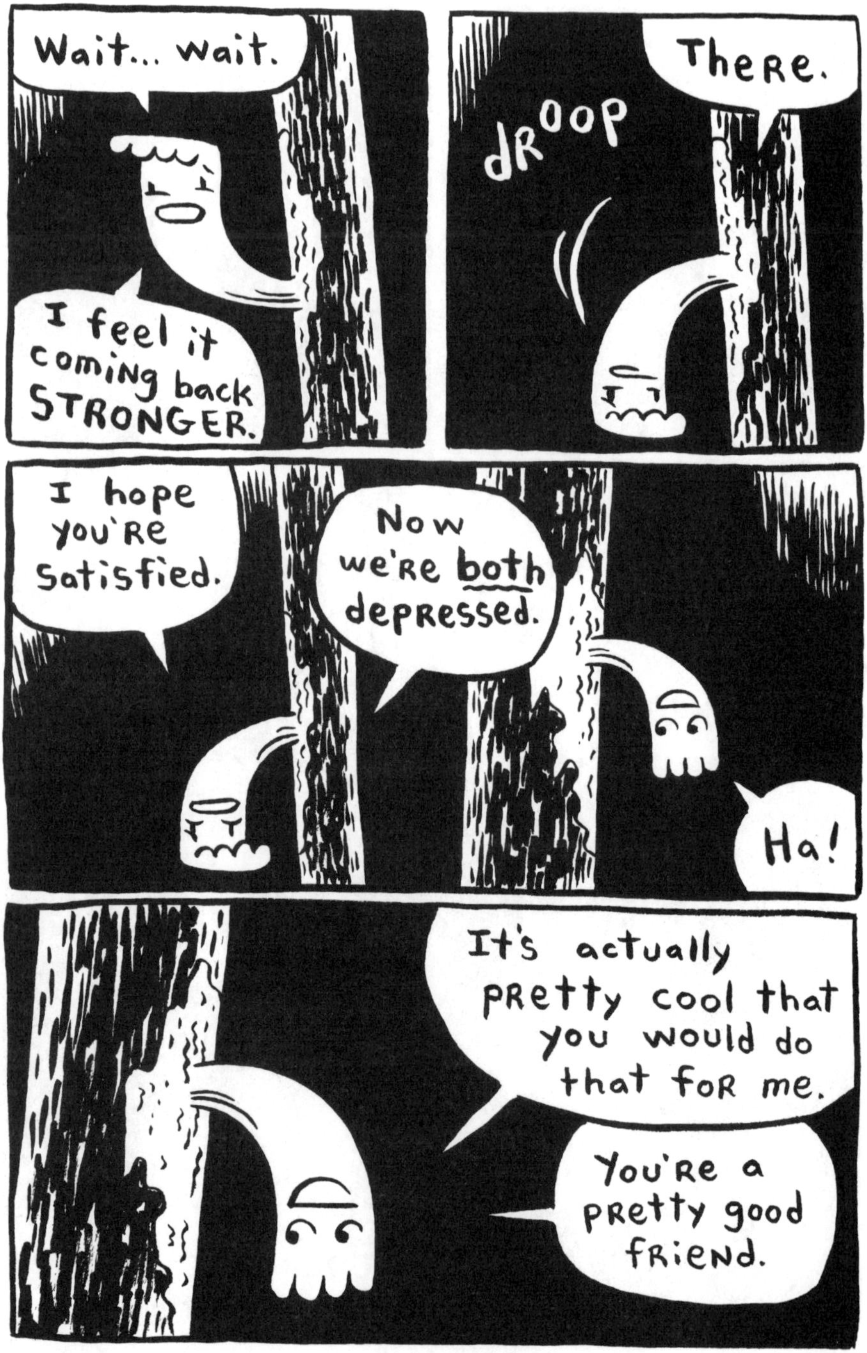
Wait... wait.
I feel it coming back STRONGER.
There.
dROOP
I hope you're satisfied.
Now we're both depressed.
Ha!
It's actually pretty cool that you would do that for me.
You're a pretty good friend.

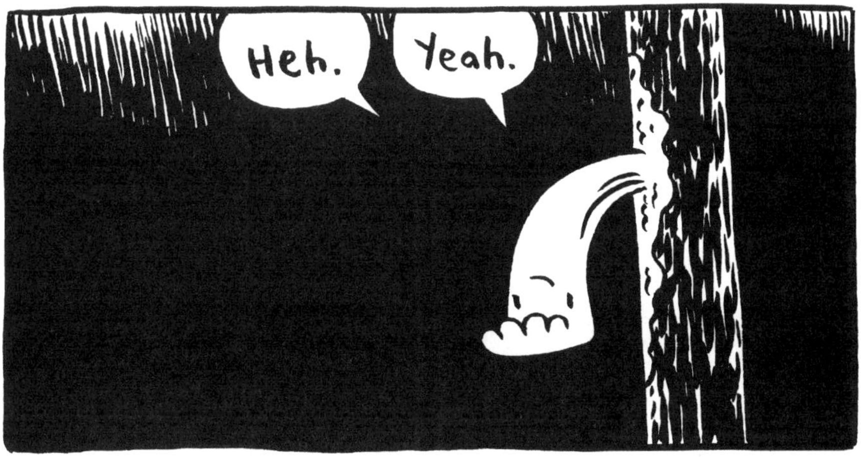
Heh.
Yeah.

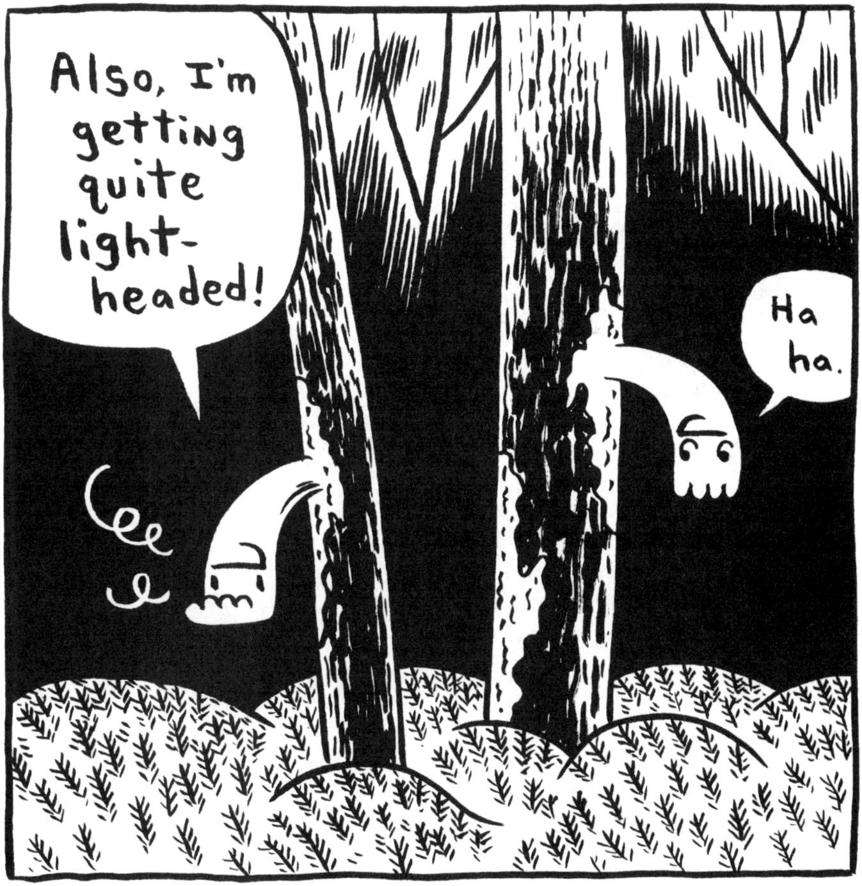
Also, I'm getting quite light-headed!
Ha ha.

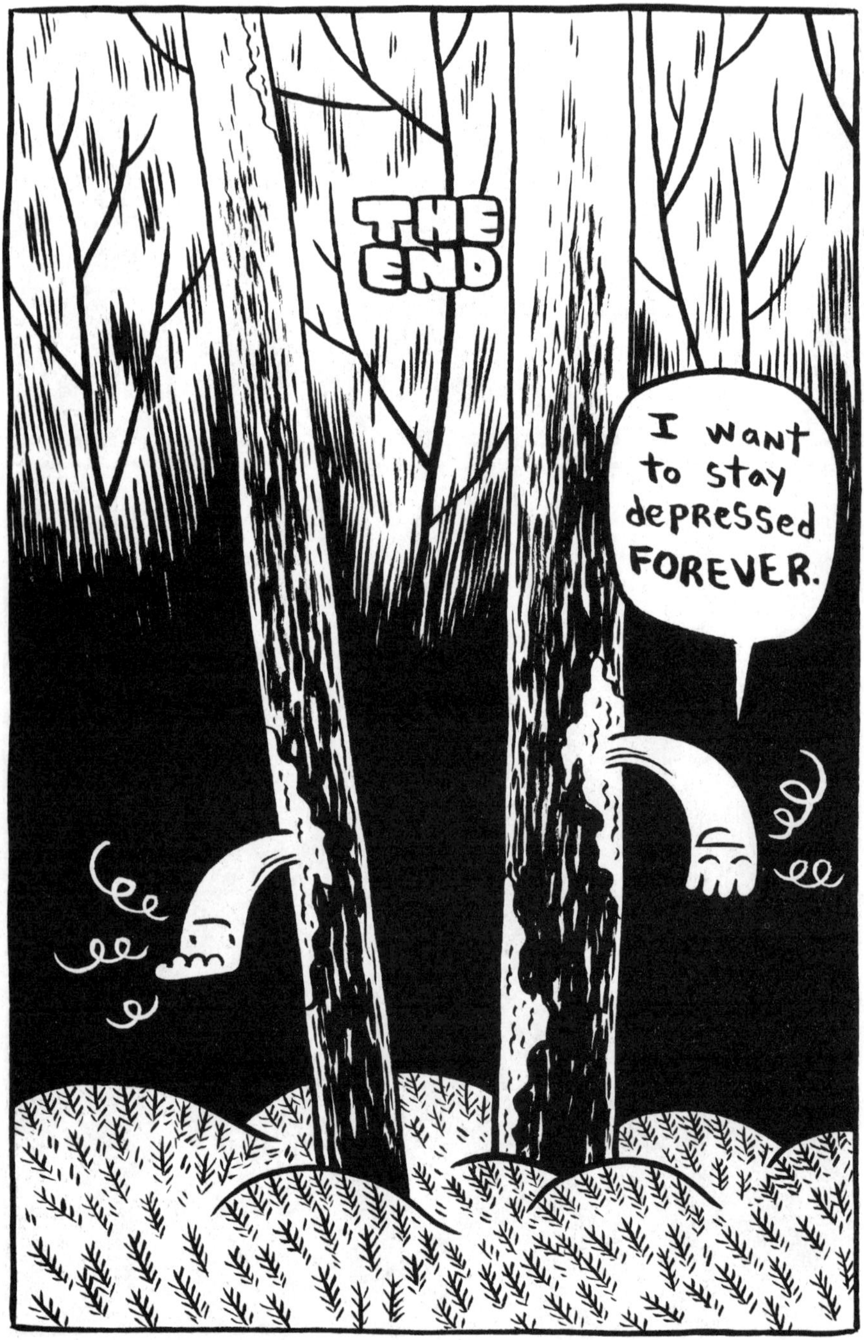
THE END
I want to stay depressed FOREVER.

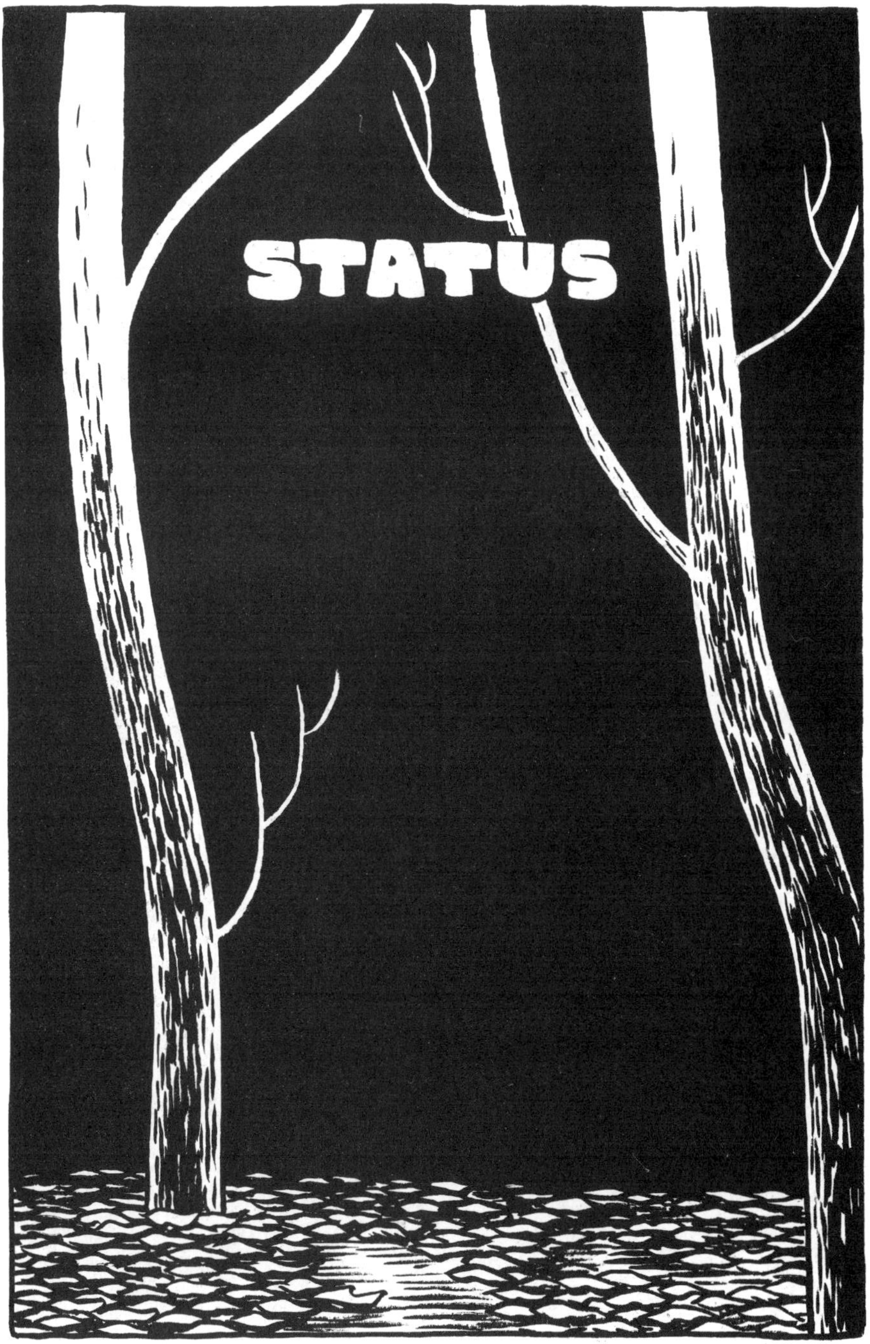
STATUS

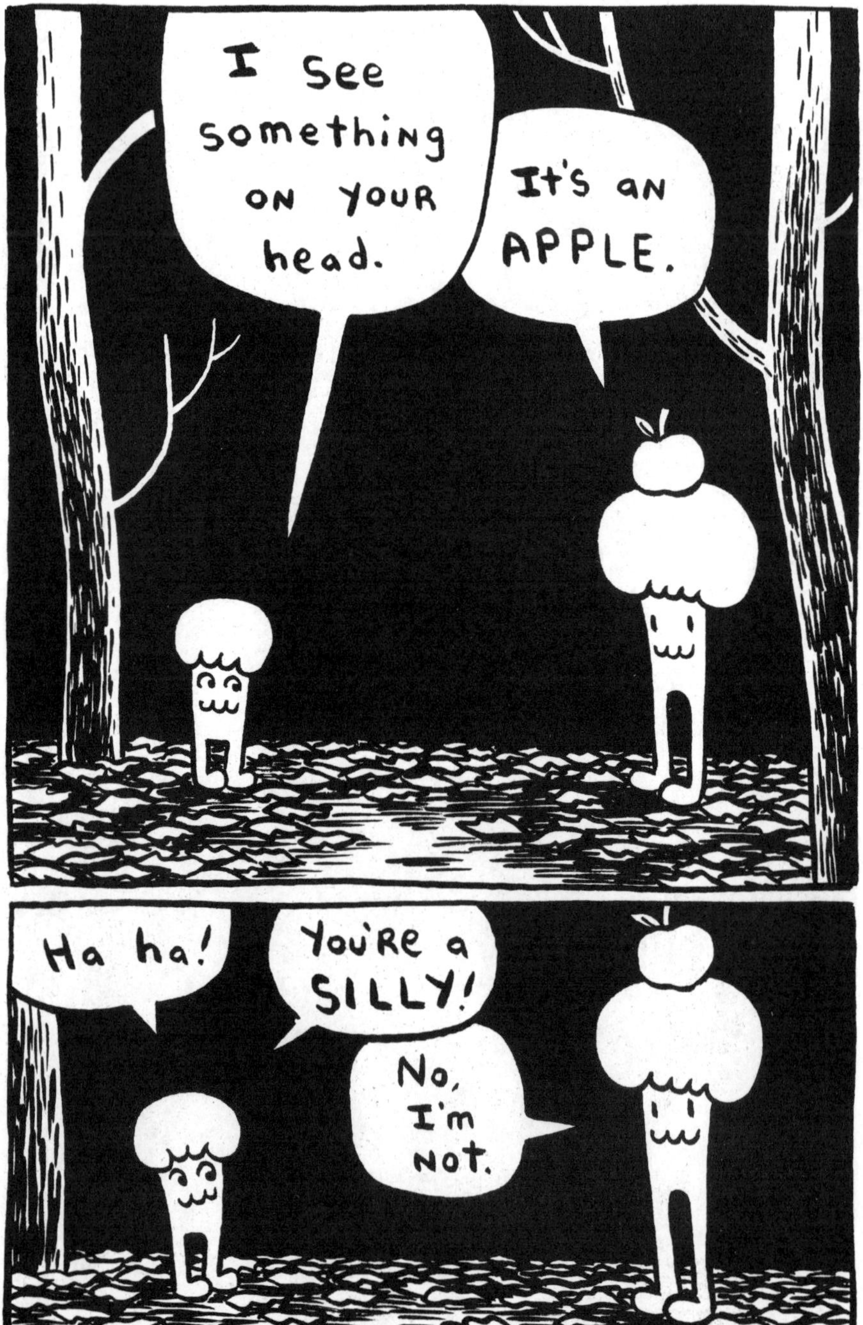
I see something on your head.
It's an APPLE.
Ha ha!
You're a SILLY!
No, I'm not.

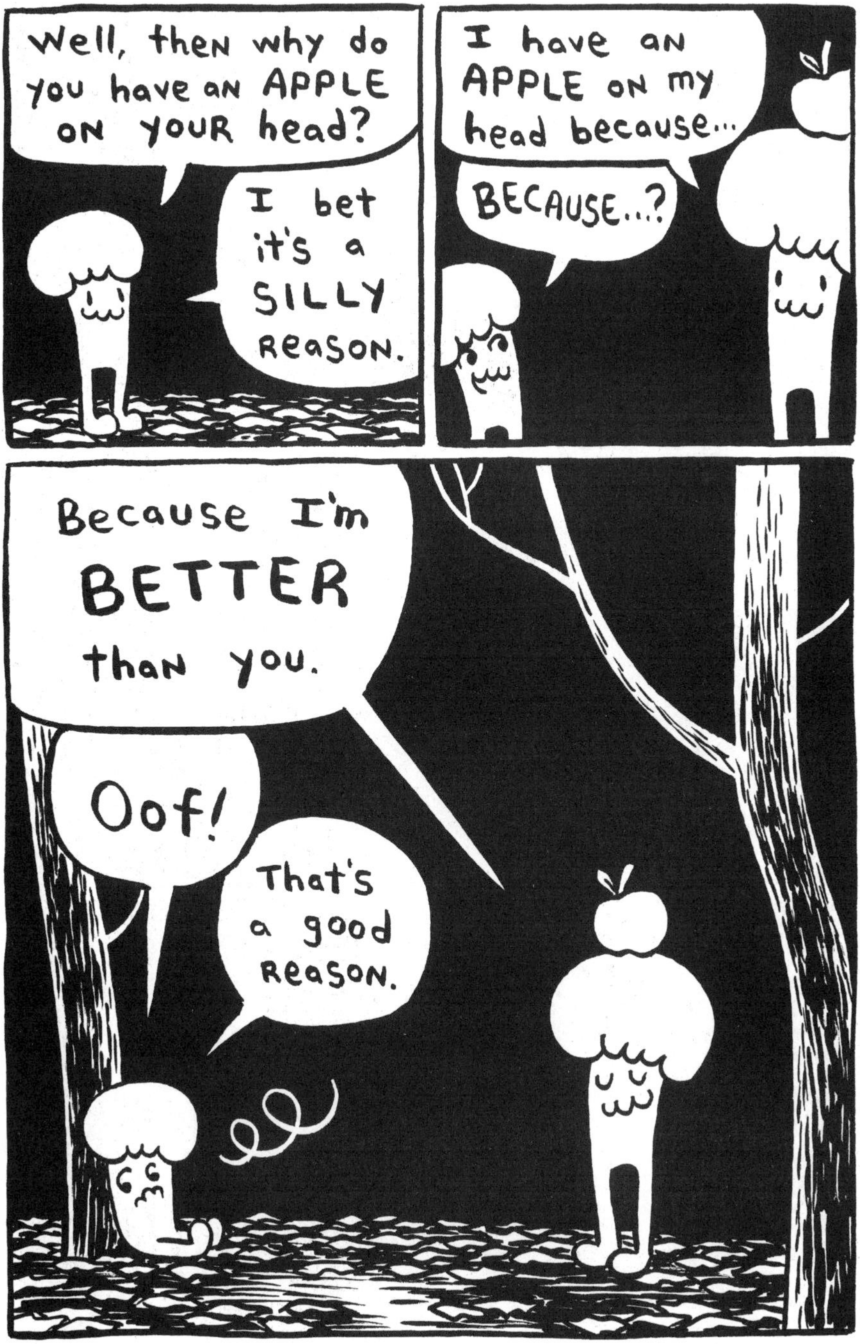
Well, then why do you have an APPLE ON YOUR head?
I bet it's a SILLY Reason.
I have an APPLE ON my head because...
BECAUSE...?
Because I'm BETTER than you.
Oof!
That's a good Reason.

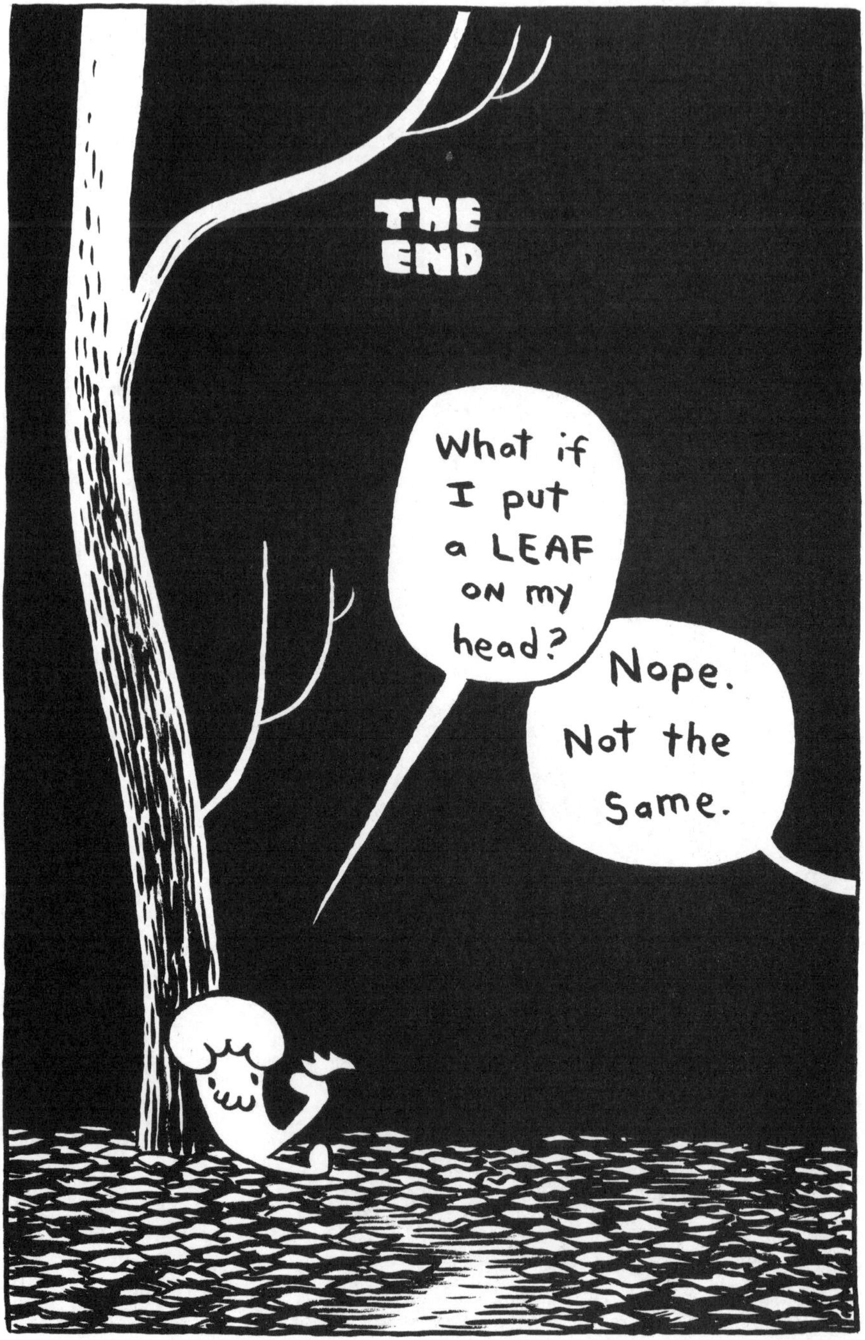
THE END
What if I put a LEAF on my head?
Nope. Not the same.

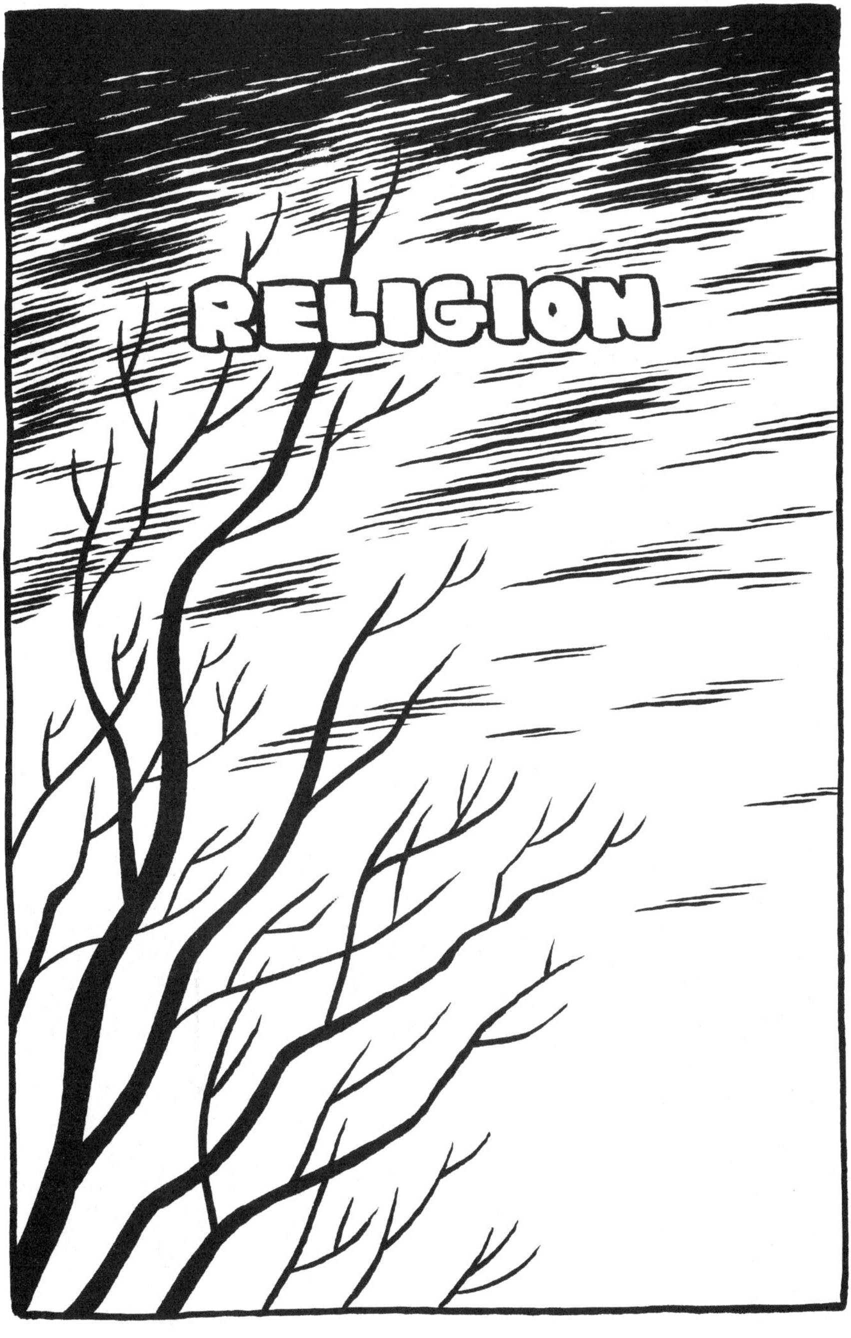
RELIGION

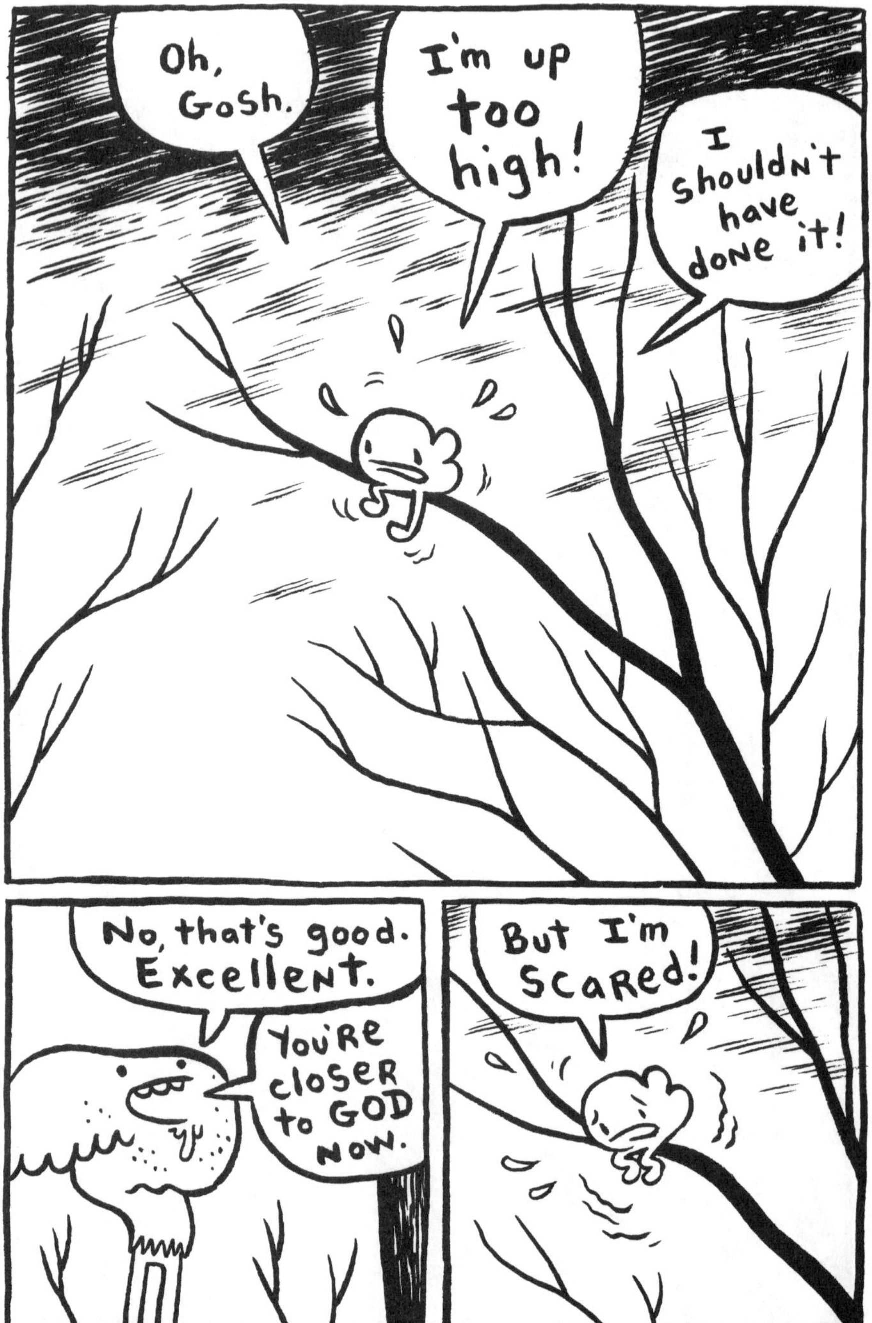
Oh, Gosh.
I'm up too high!
I shouldn't have done it!
No, that's good. Excellent.
You're closer to GOD now.
But I'm scared!

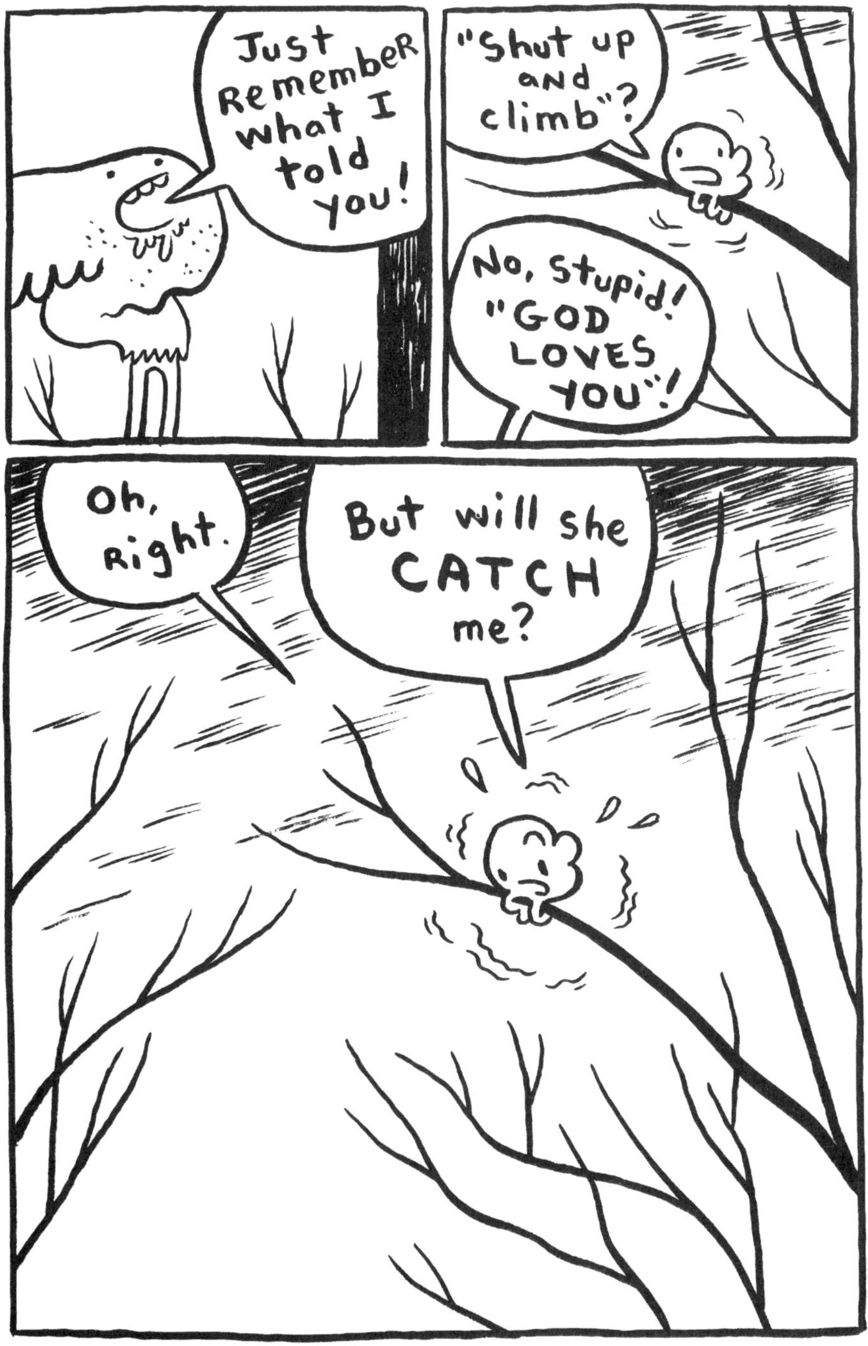
Just Remember what I told you!
"Shut up and climb"?
No, stupid! "GOD LOVES YOU"!
Oh, Right.
But will she CATCH me?

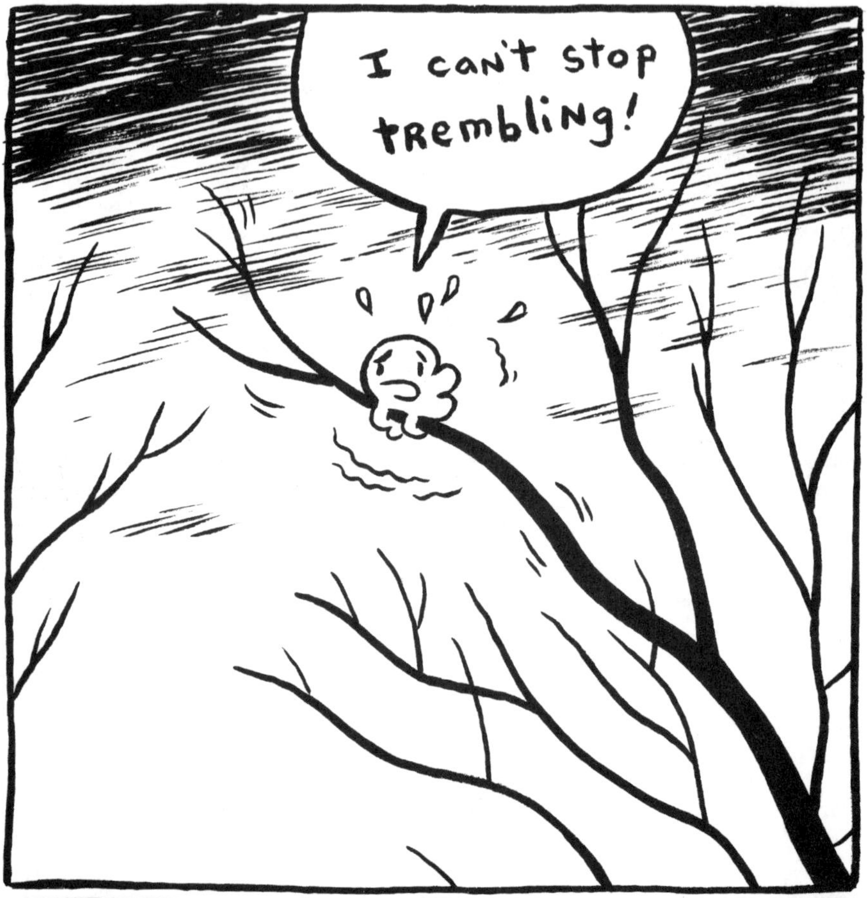
I can't stop trembling!

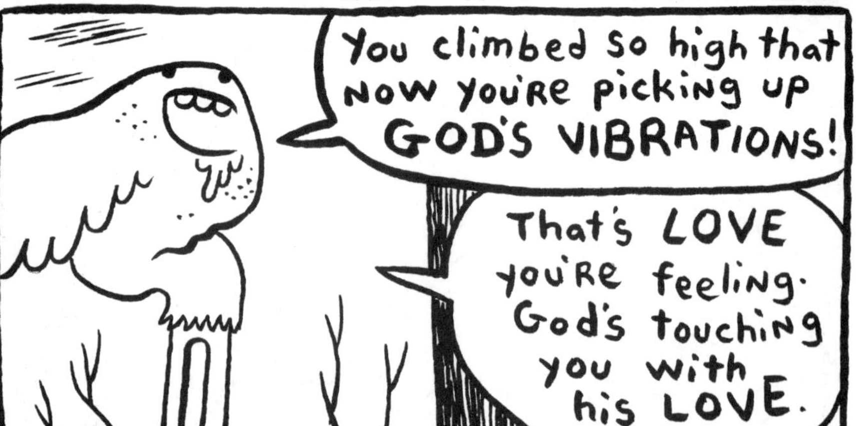
You climbed so high that now you're picking up GOD'S VIBRATIONS!
That's LOVE you're feeling. God's touching you with his LOVE.

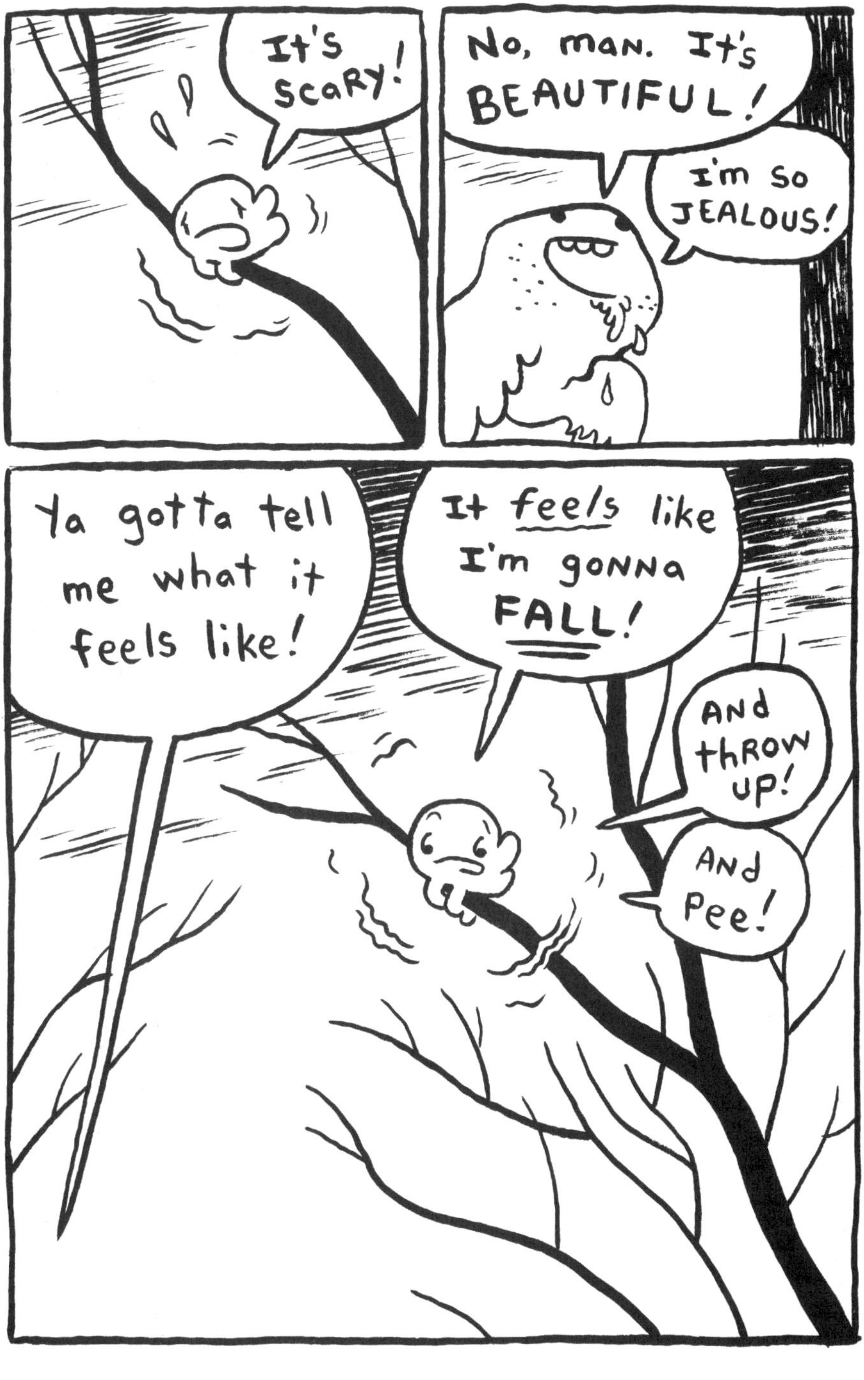
It's scary!
No, man. It's BEAUTIFUL!
I'm so JEALOUS!
Ya gotta tell me what it feels like!
It feels like I'm gonna FALL!
And throw up!
And pee!

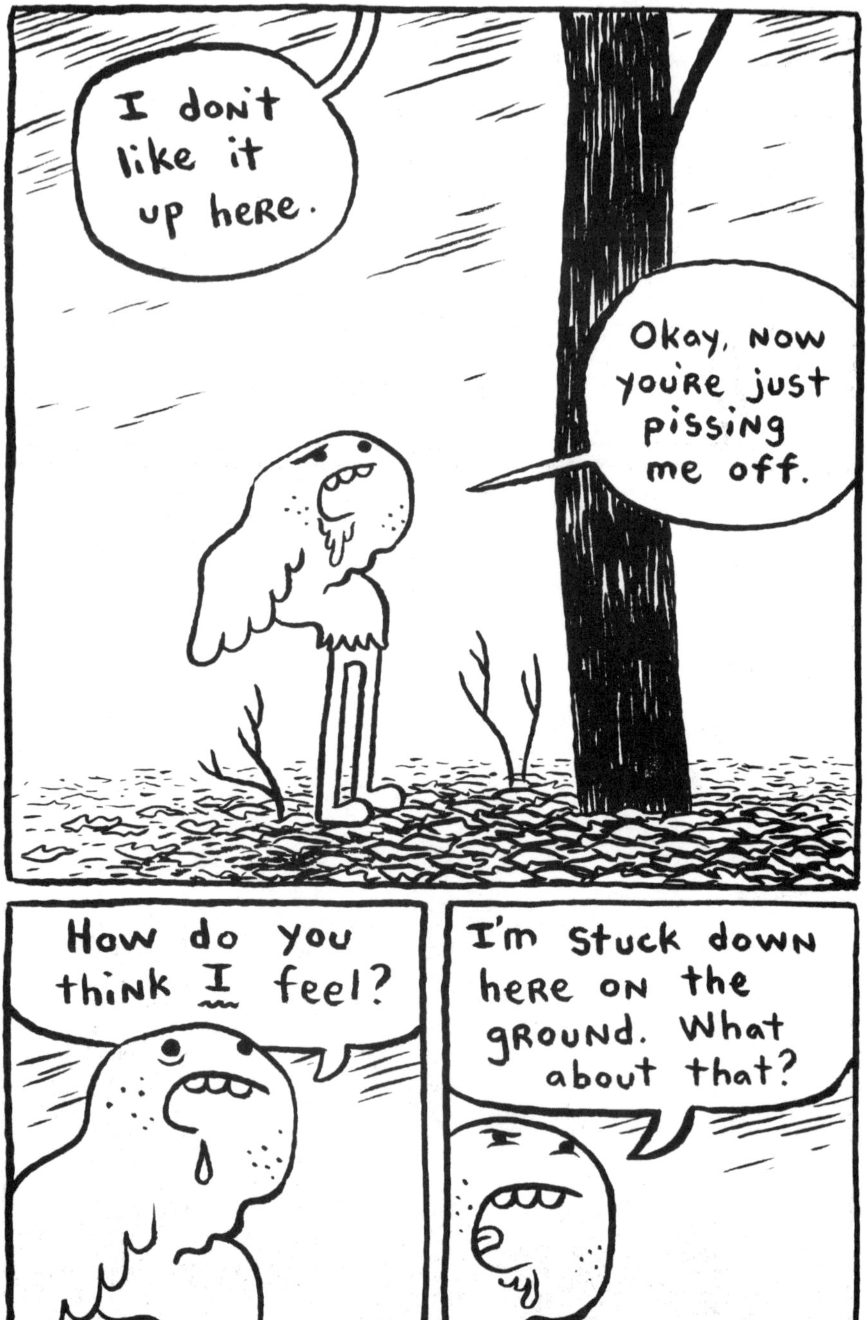
I don't like it up here.
Okay, now you're just pissing me off.
How do you think I feel?
I'm stuck down here on the ground. What about that?

You think just because you're way up there you're better than me!?
No!
I didn't say that!
Maybe God put you up there because he wants ME to knock you down!
BAM
Hey!
Don't!

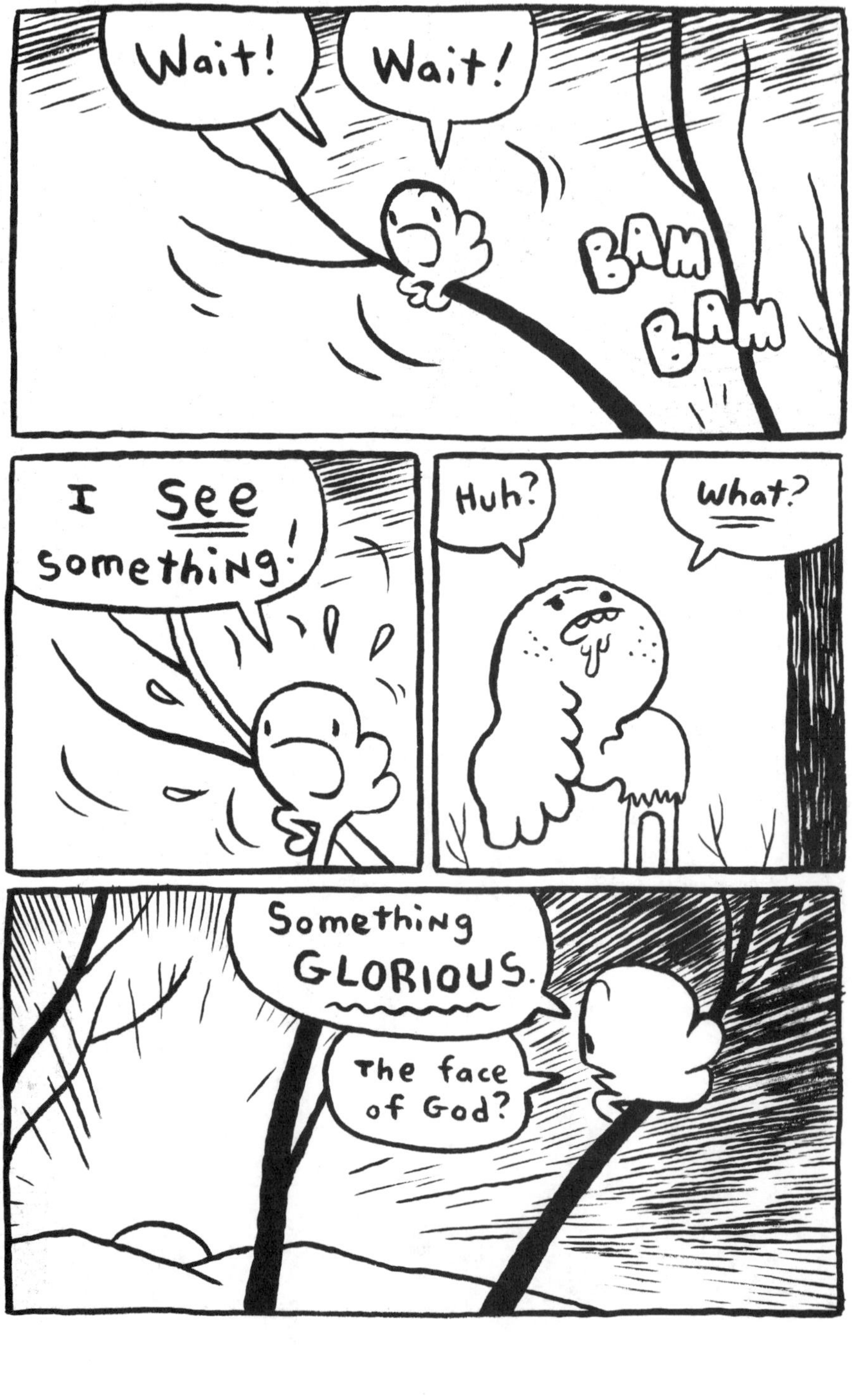
Wait!
Wait!
BAM BAM
I see something!
Huh?
What?
Something GLORIOUS.
The face of God?

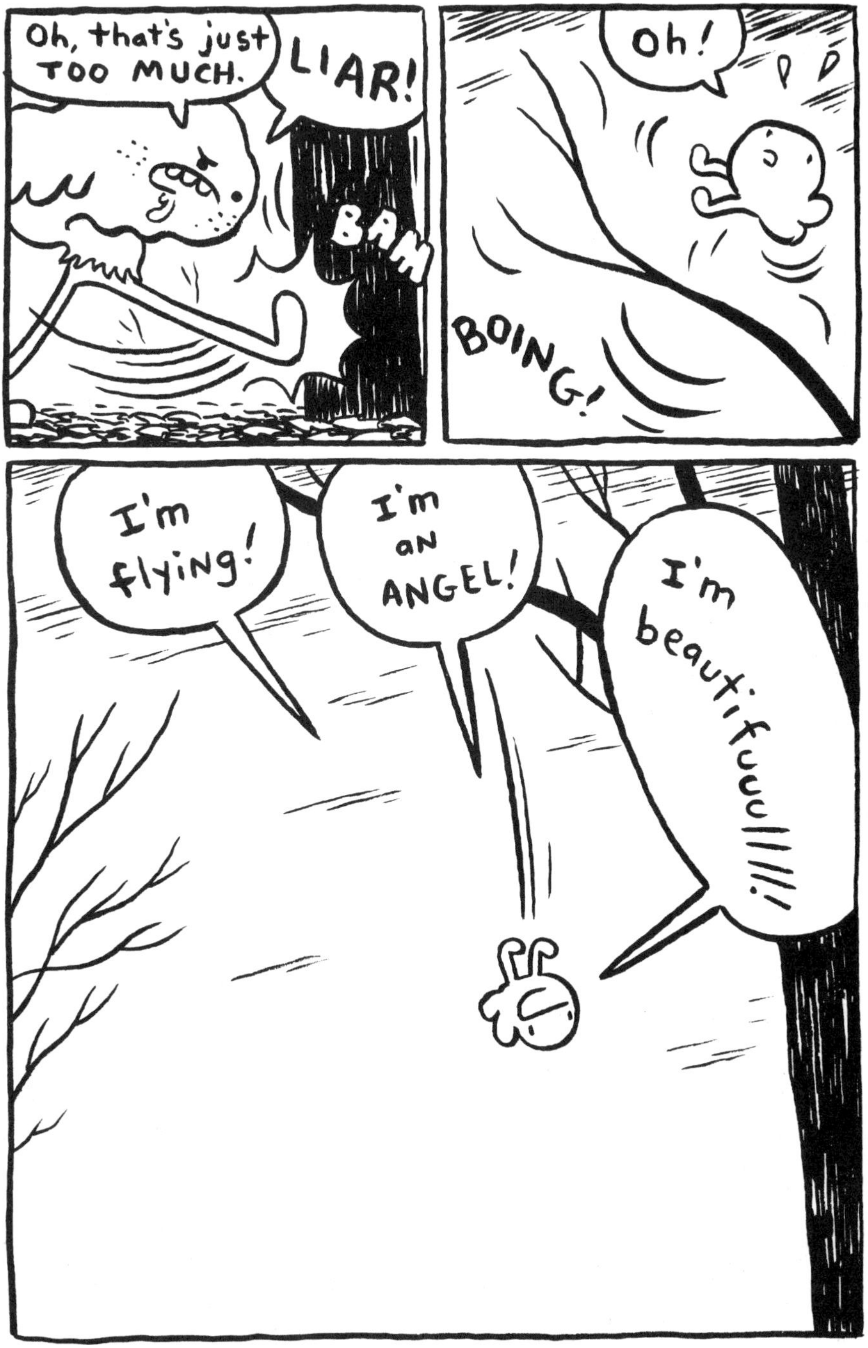
Oh, that's just TOO MUCH.
LIAR!
BAM
Oh!
BOING!
I'm flying!
I'm an ANGEL!
I'm beautifuuu!!!!!

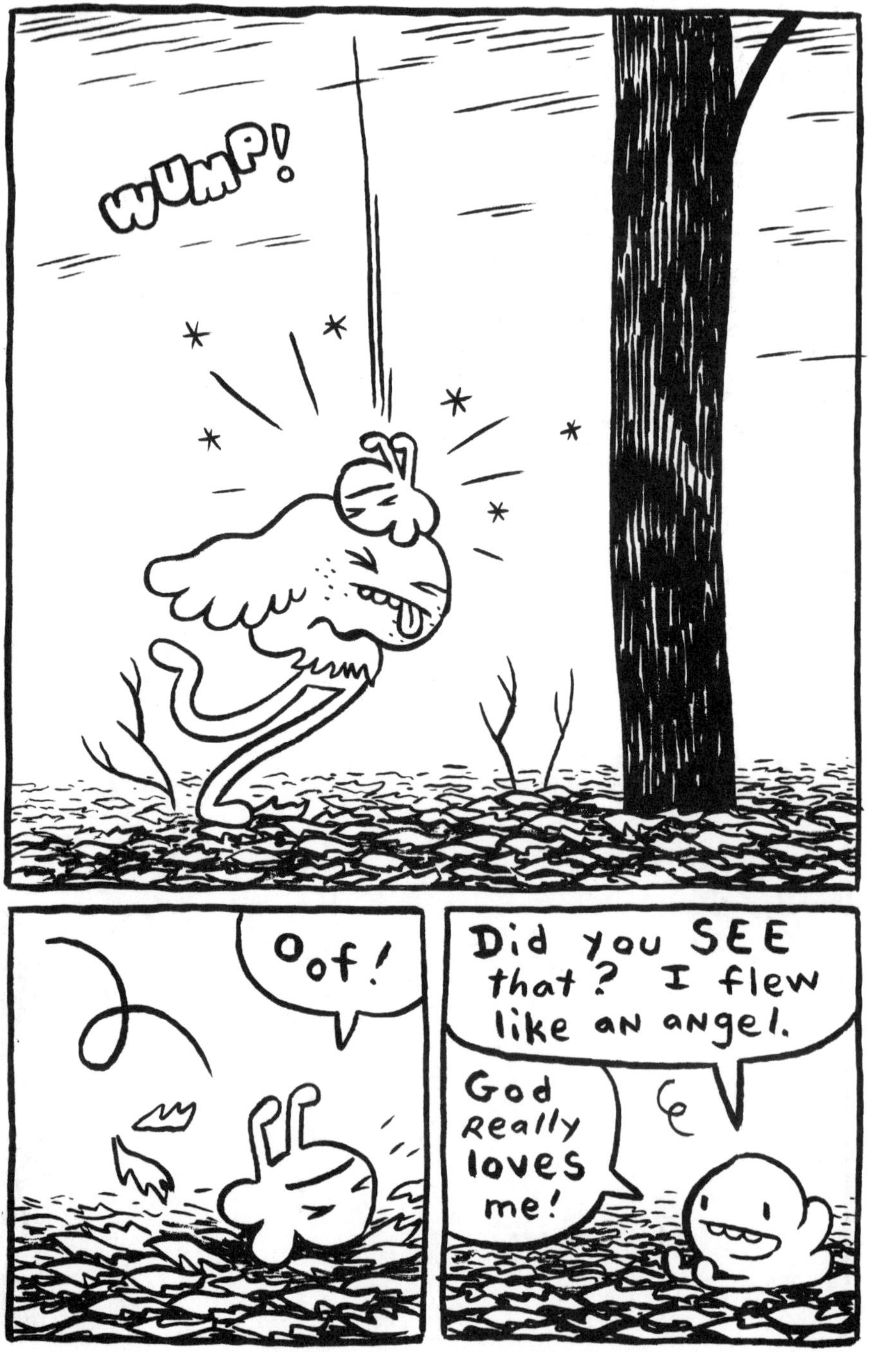
WUMP!
Oof!
Did you SEE that? I flew like an angel.
God really loves me!

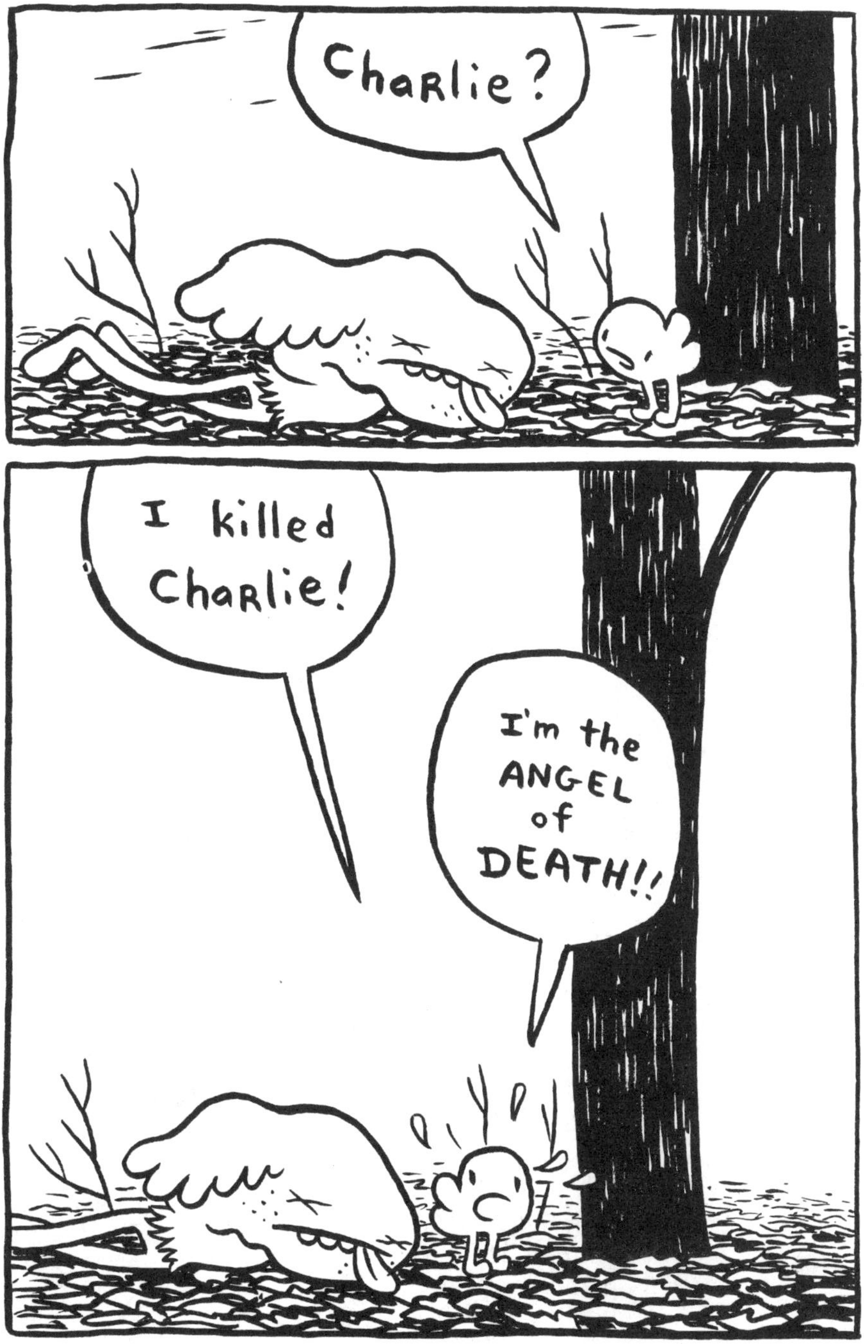
Charlie?
I killed Charlie!
I'm the ANGEL of DEATH!!

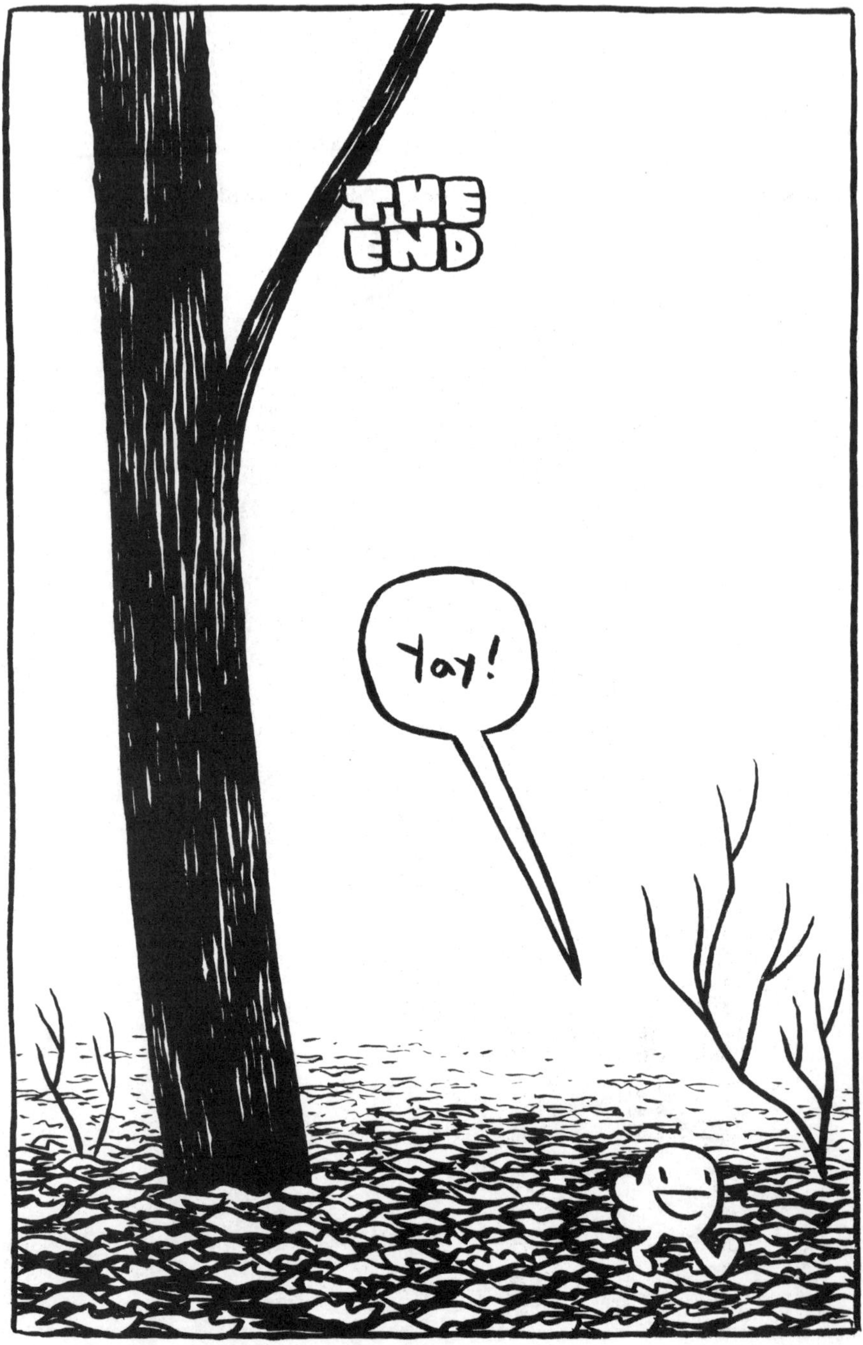
THE END
Yay!

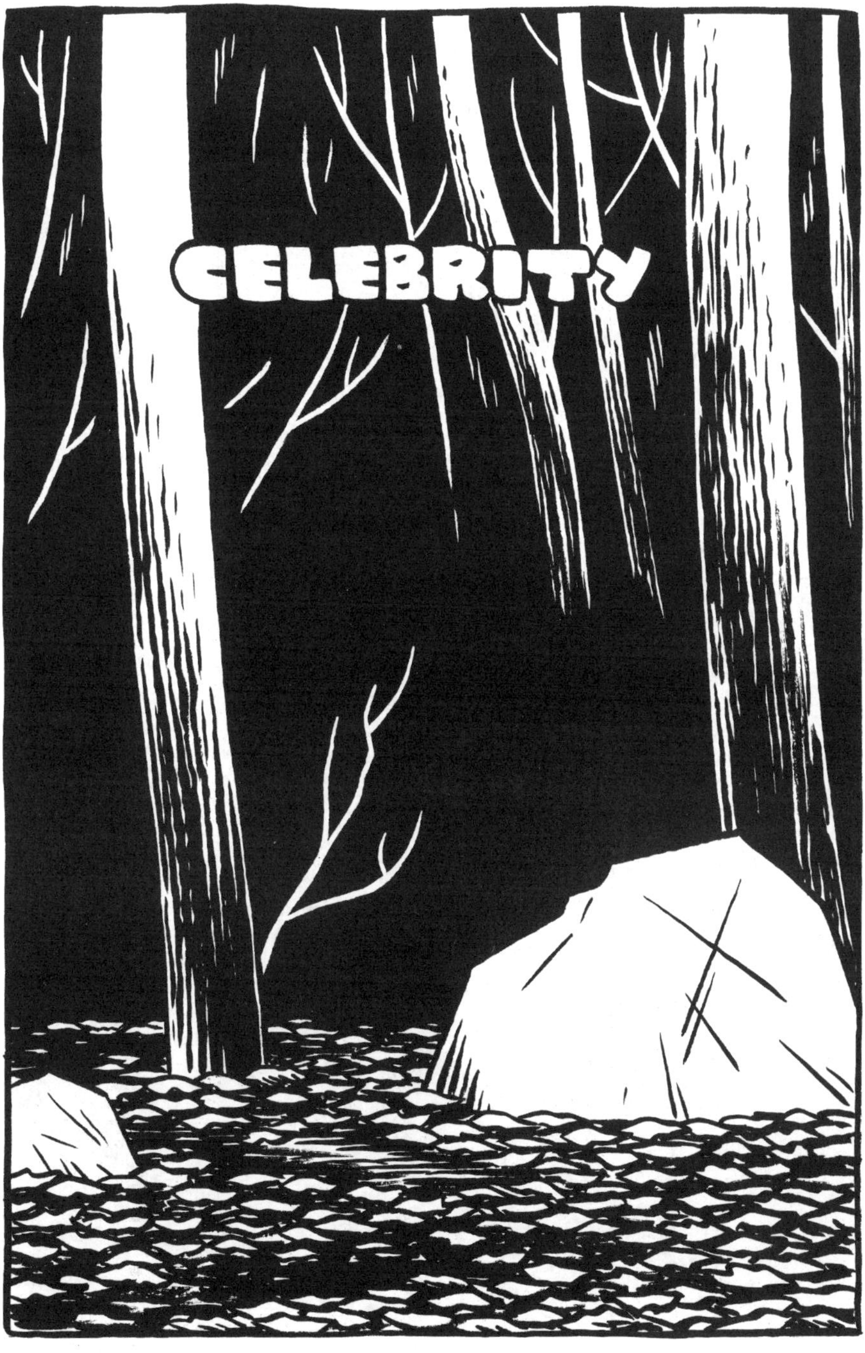
CELEBRITY

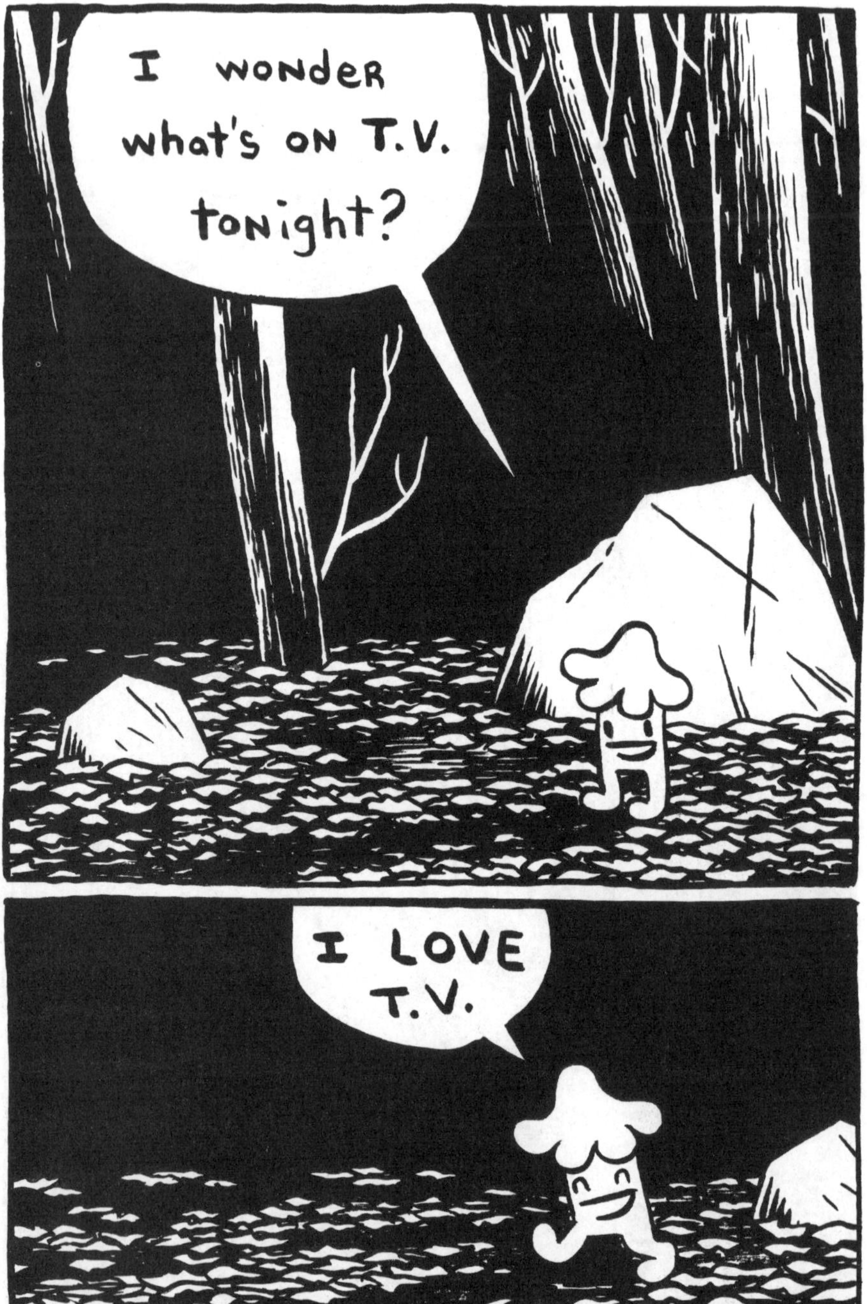
I wonder what's on T.V. tonight?
I LOVE T.V.

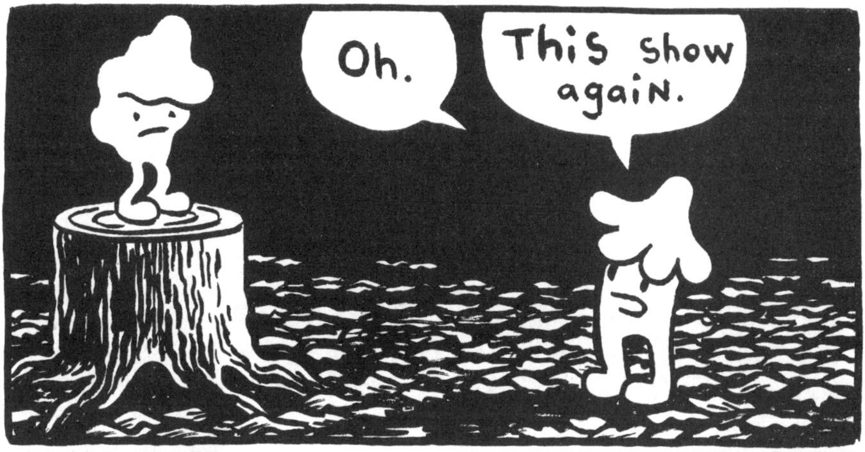
Oh.
This show again.

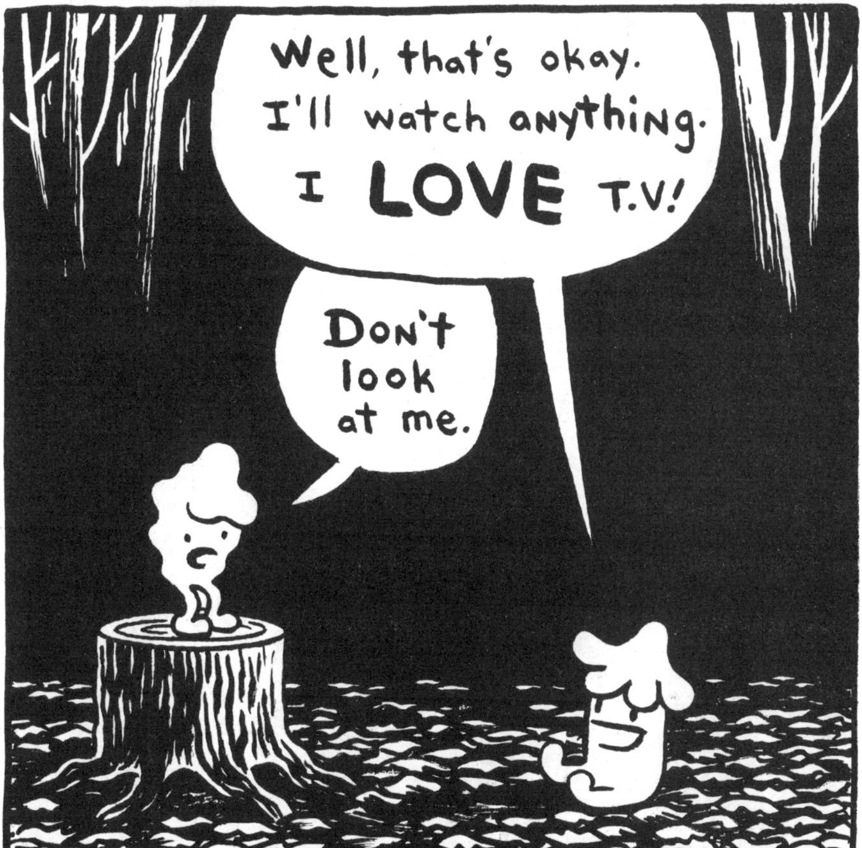
Well, that's okay. I'll watch anything. I LOVE T.V!
Don't look at me.

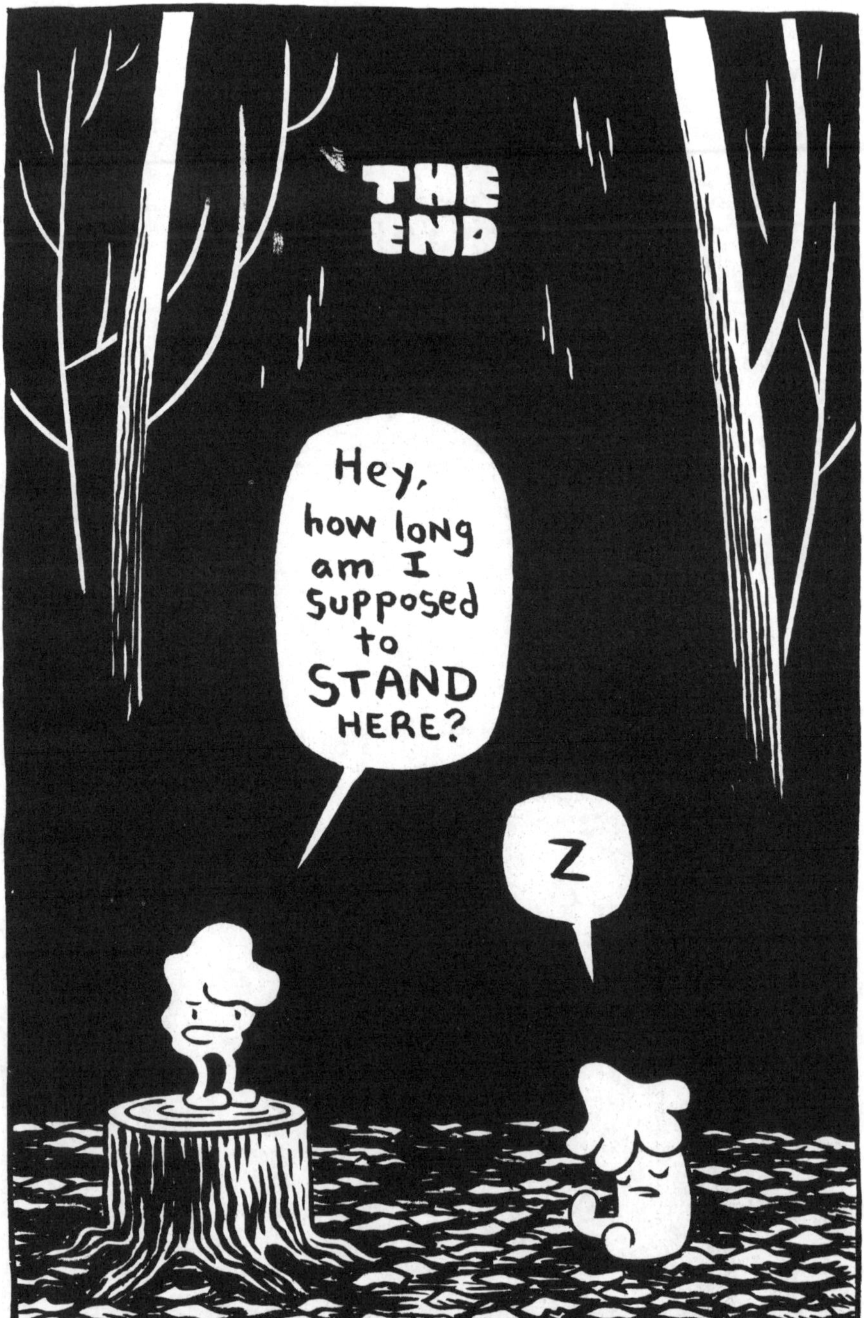
THE END
Hey, how long am I supposed to STAND HERE?
Z

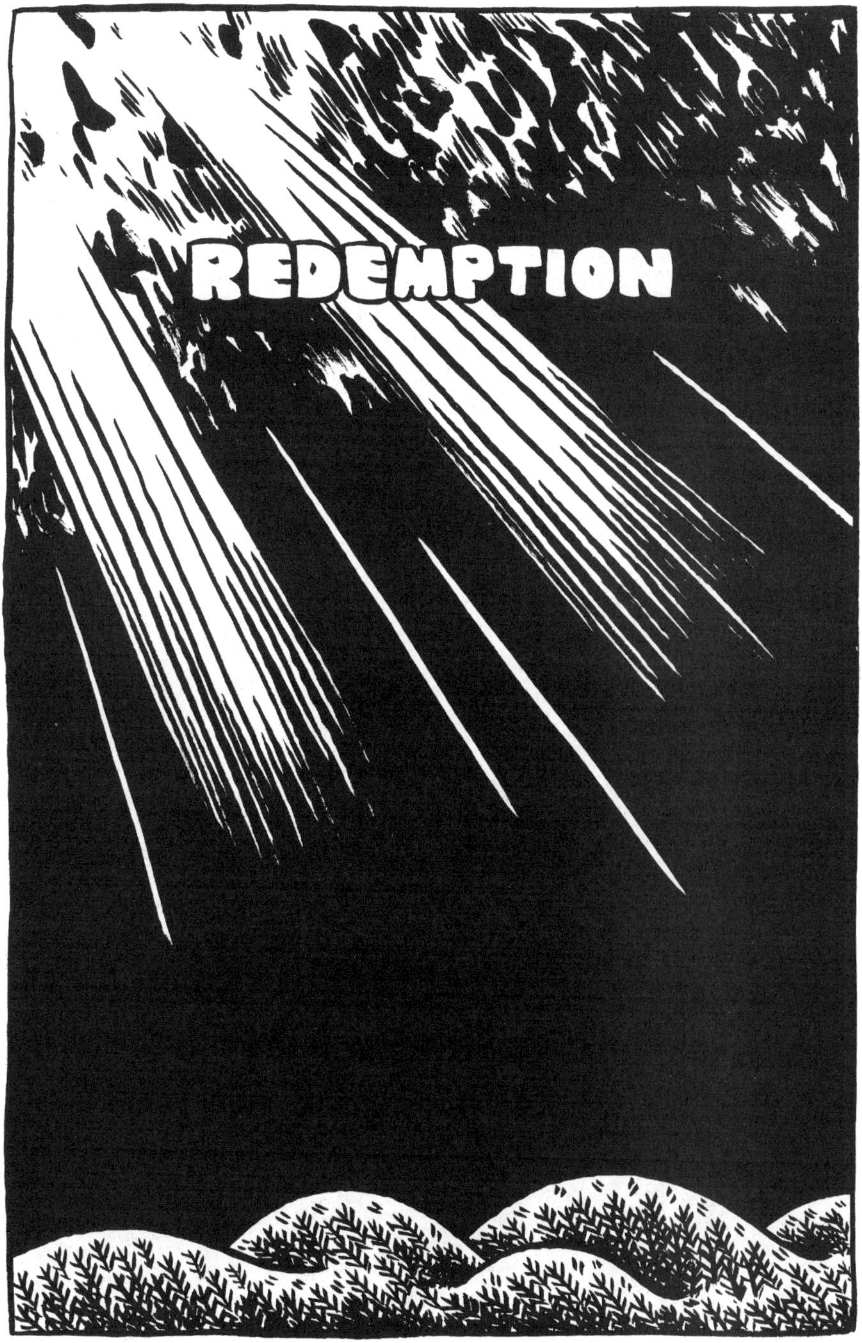
REDEMPTION

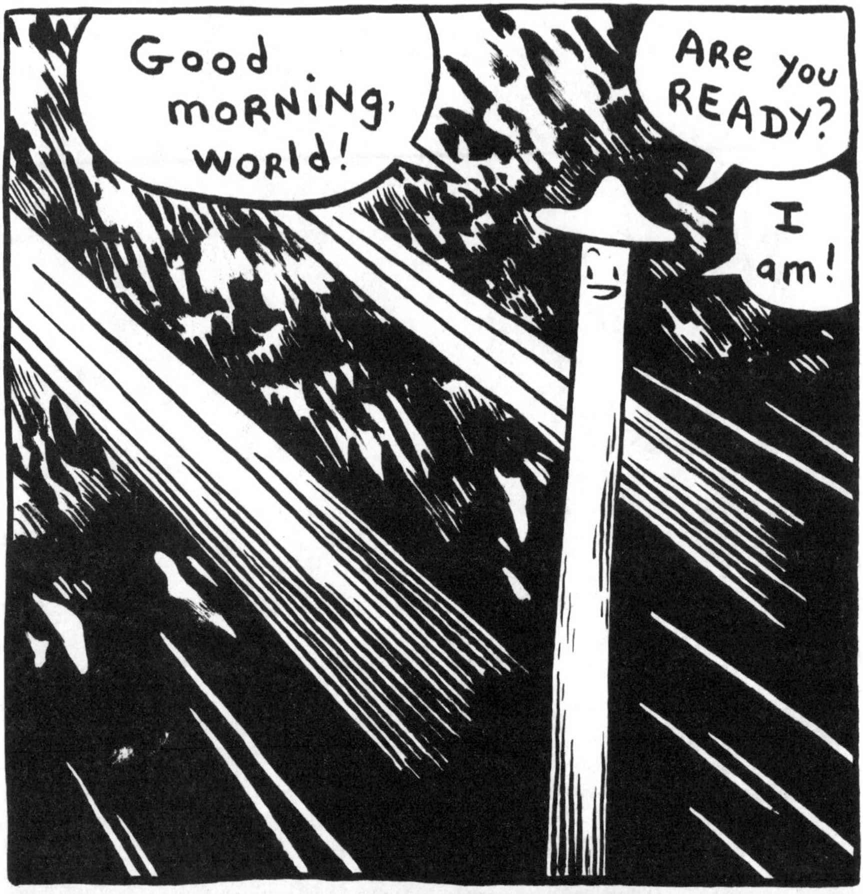
Good morning, world!
Are you READY?
I am!

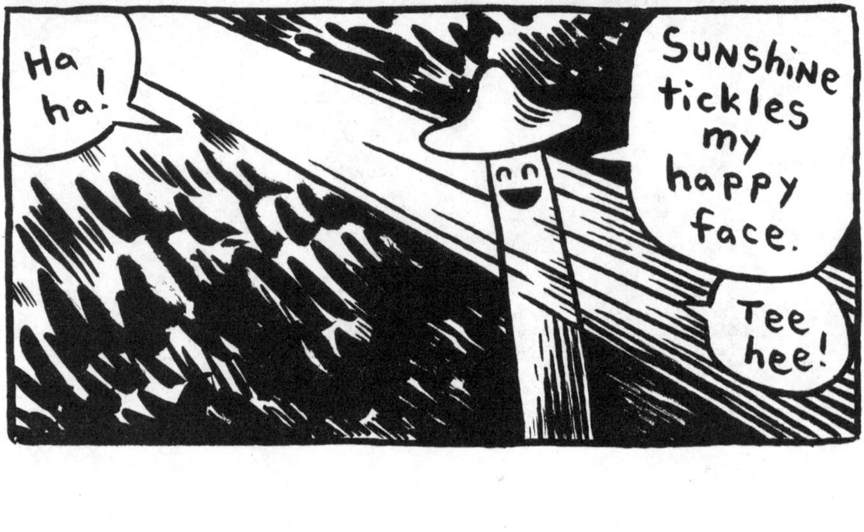
Ha ha!
Sunshine tickles my happy face.
Tee hee!

But... I wonder if my feet ever get LONELY way down there in the Shadows.

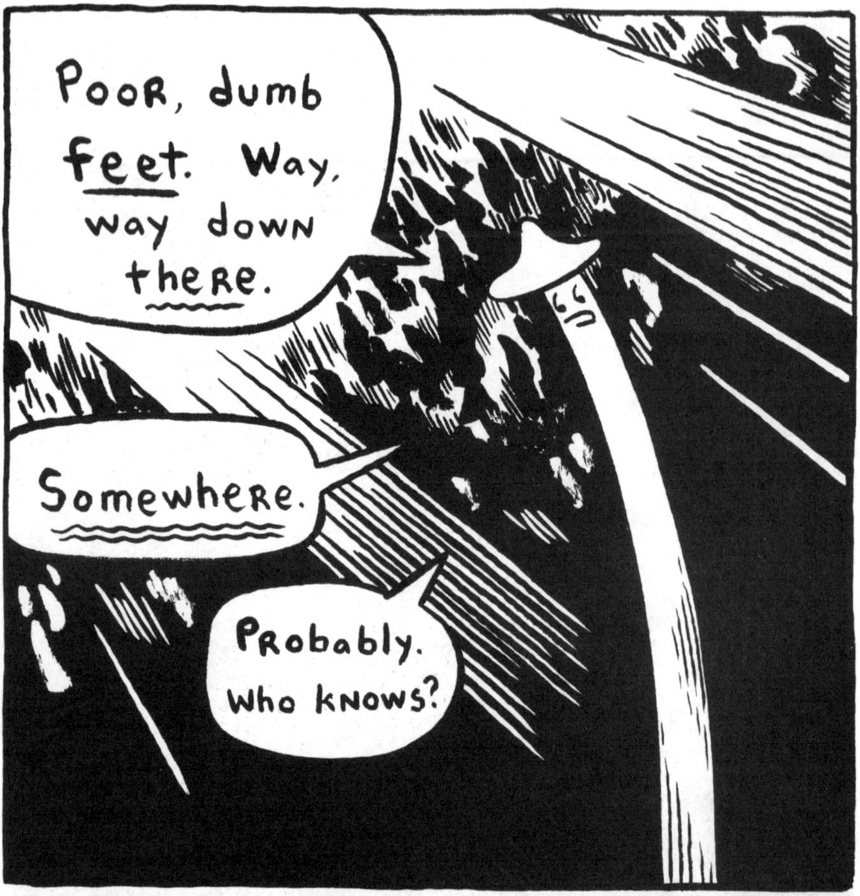
Poor, dumb feet. Way, way down there.
Somewhere.
Probably. Who knows?

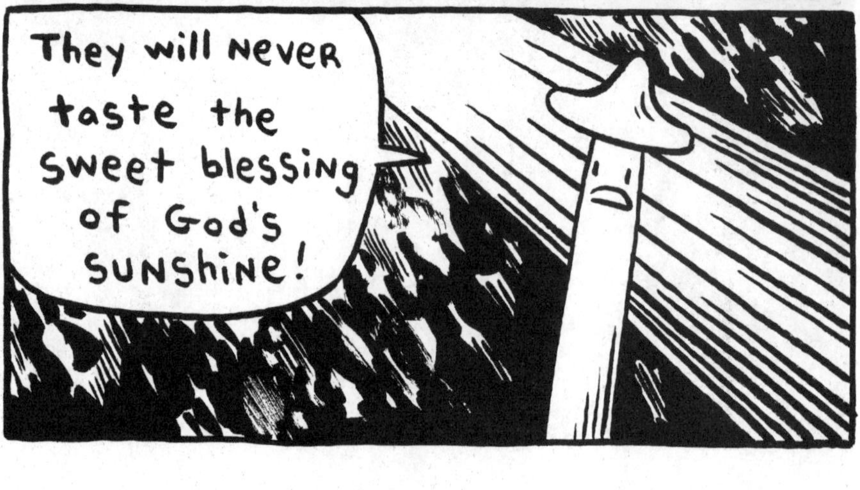
They will never taste the sweet blessing of God's sunshine!

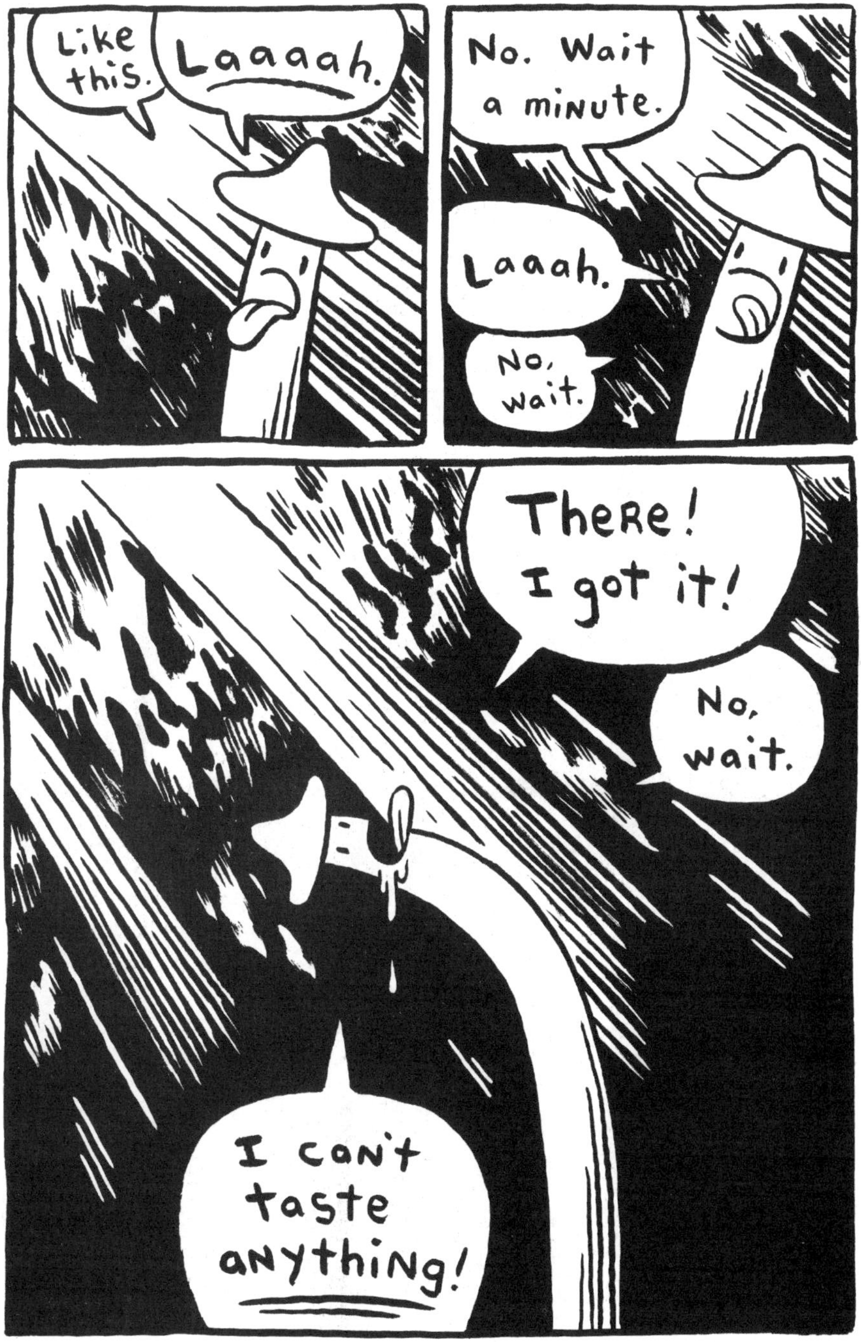
Like this.
Laaaah.
No. Wait a minute.
Laaah.
No, wait.
There! I got it!
No, wait.
I can't taste anything!

I can't taste the SUNSHINE!?
NO, NO, NO!

Why, GOD, why?
Why have you FORSaken my tongue?!

Dude, you're so LUCKY!
Laah?
Yeah. God hates you.
Now you've got a GREAT excuse to update your FACEBOOK status!

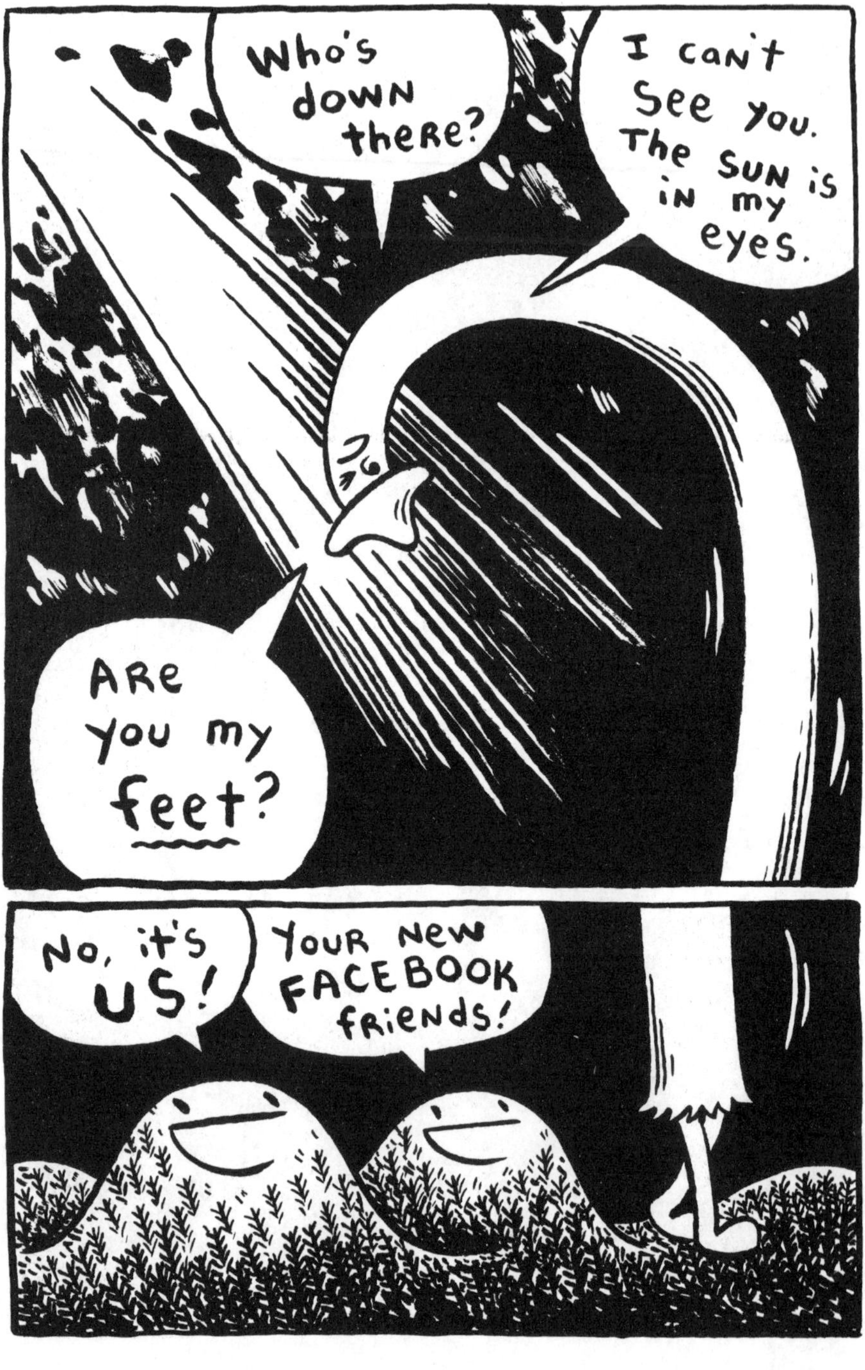
Who's down there?
I can't See you. The SUN is in my eyes.
ARe you my feet?
No, it's US!
YOUR New FACEBOOK friends!

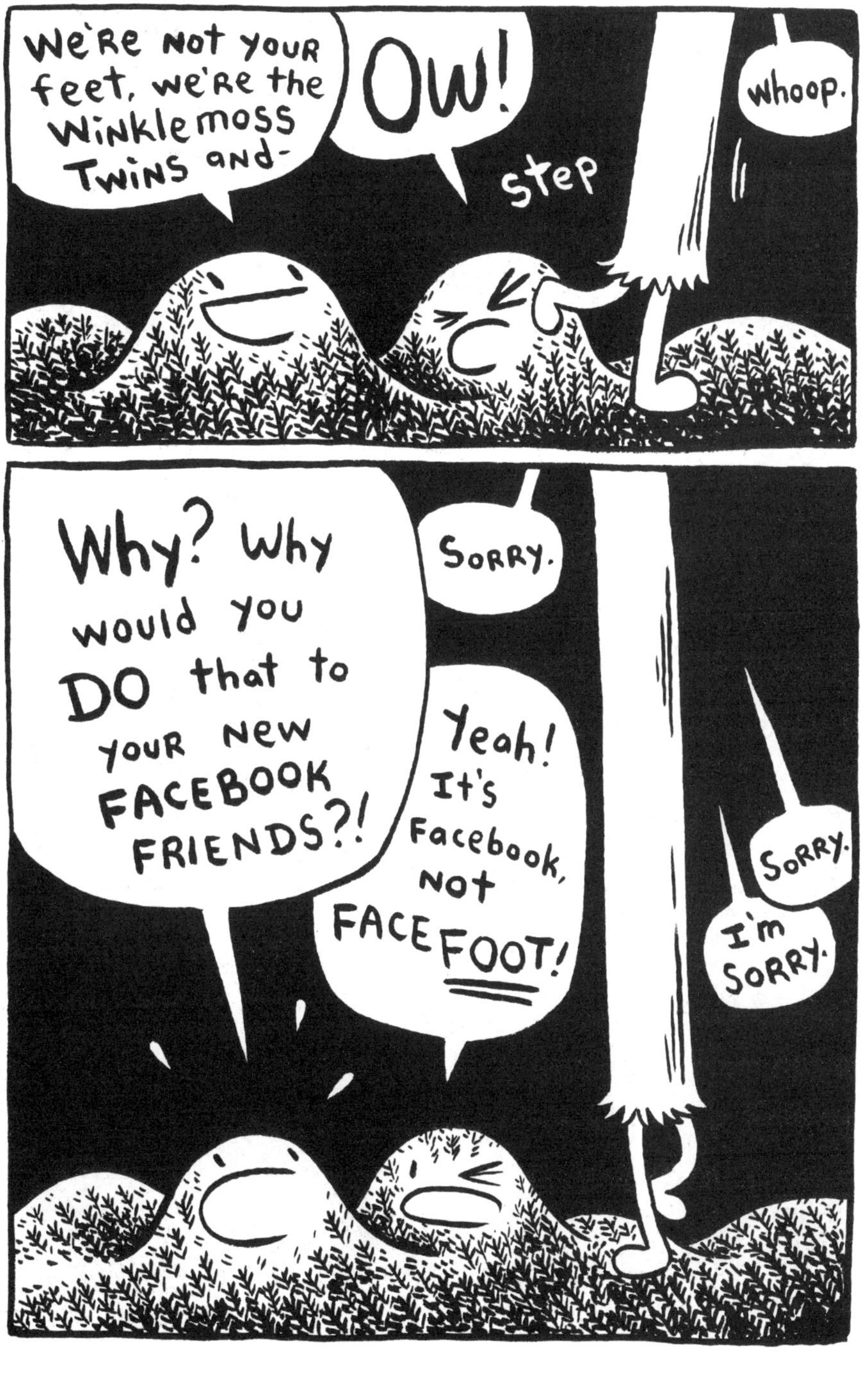
We're not your feet, we're the Winklemoss Twins and-
Ow!
step
whoop.
Why? Why would you DO that to your new FACEBOOK FRIENDS?!
SORRY.
Yeah! It's Facebook, not FACEFOOT!
SORRY.
I'm SORRY.

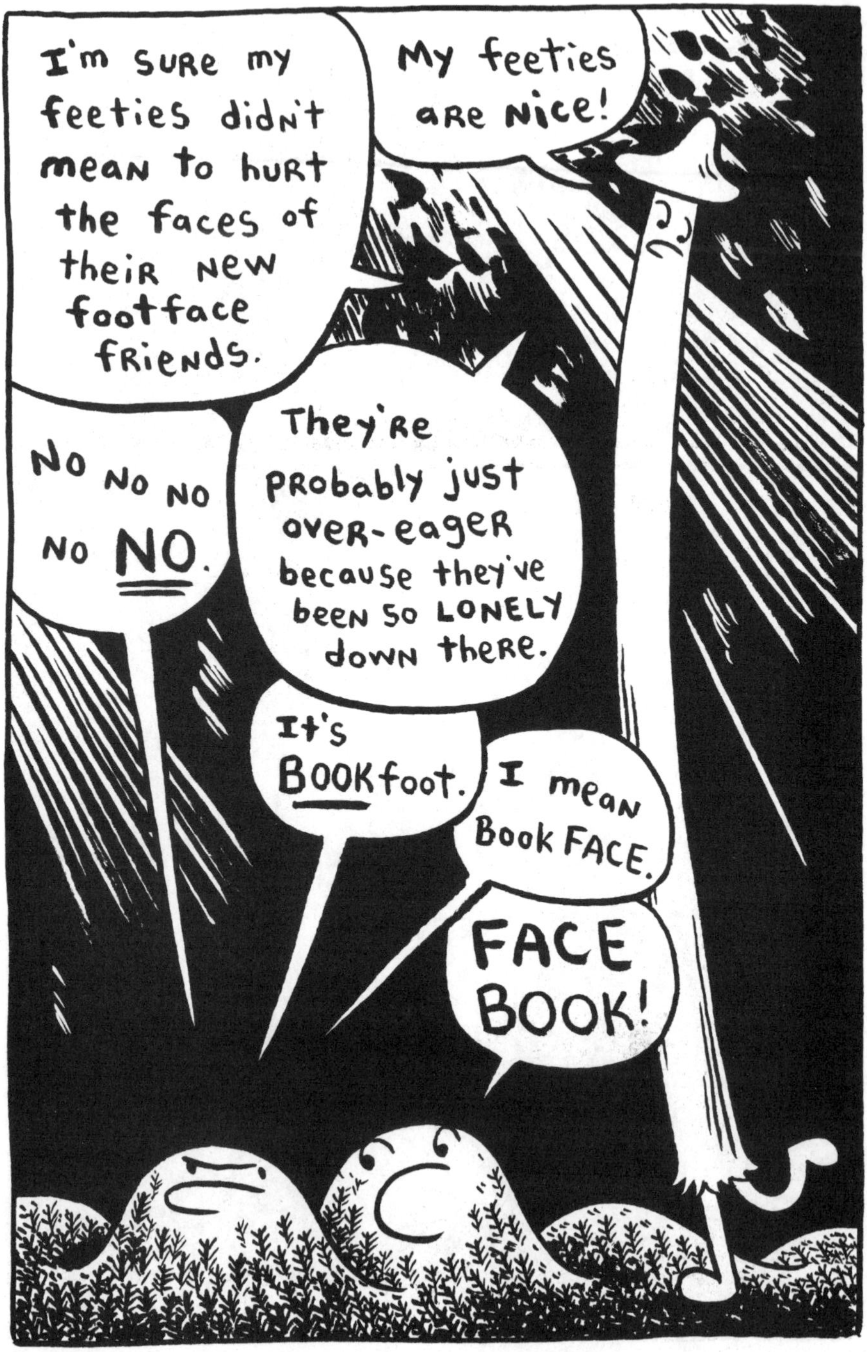
I'm sure my feeties didn't mean to hurt the faces of their new footface friends.
My feeties are nice!
No no no no NO.
They're probably just over-eager because they've been so LONELY down there.
It's BOOKfoot.
I mean Book FACE.
FACE BOOK!

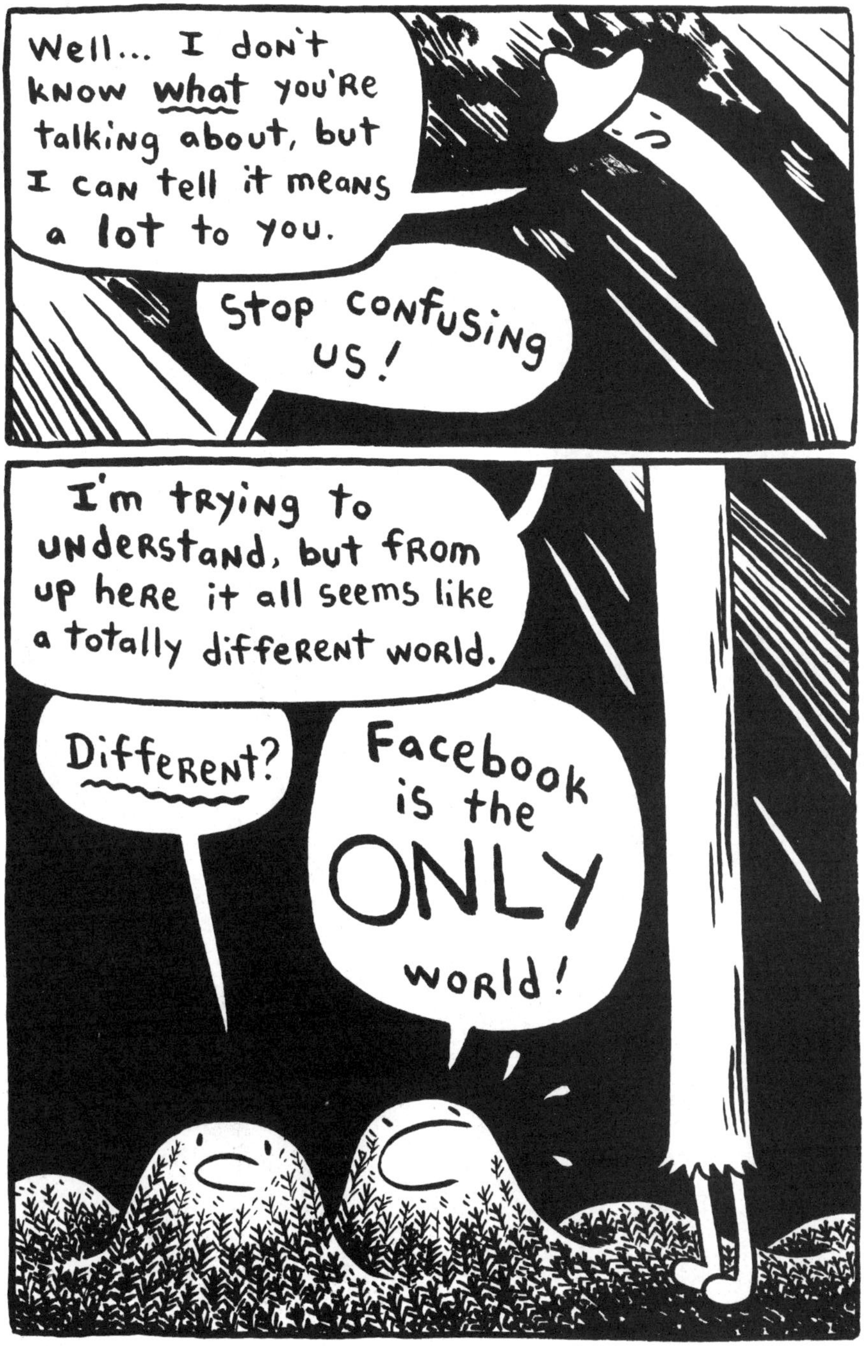
Well... I don't know what you're talking about, but I can tell it means a lot to you.
Stop confusing us!
I'm trying to understand, but from up here it all seems like a totally different world.
Different?
Facebook is the ONLY world!

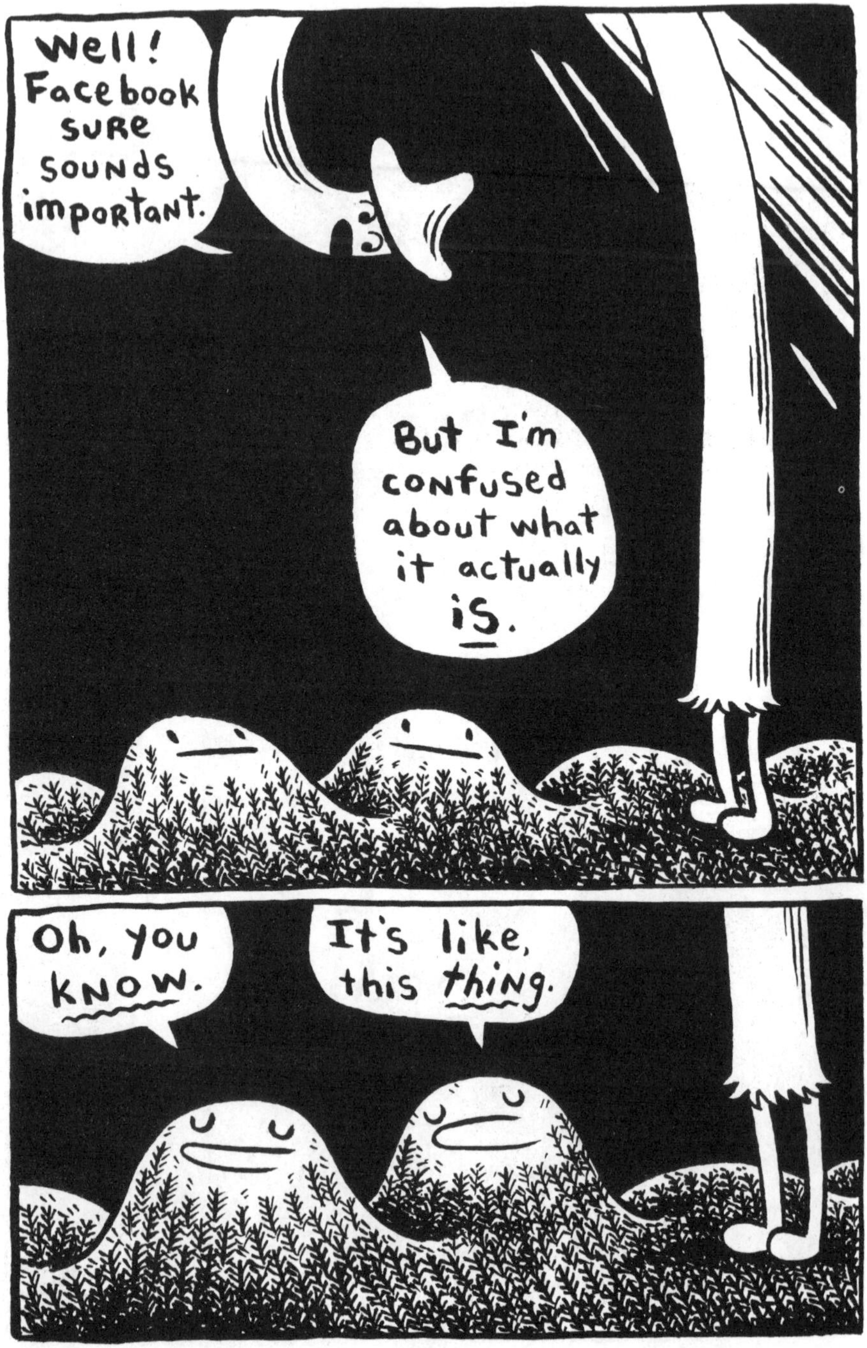
Well! Facebook sure sounds important.
But I'm confused about what it actually is.
Oh, you know.
It's like, this thing.

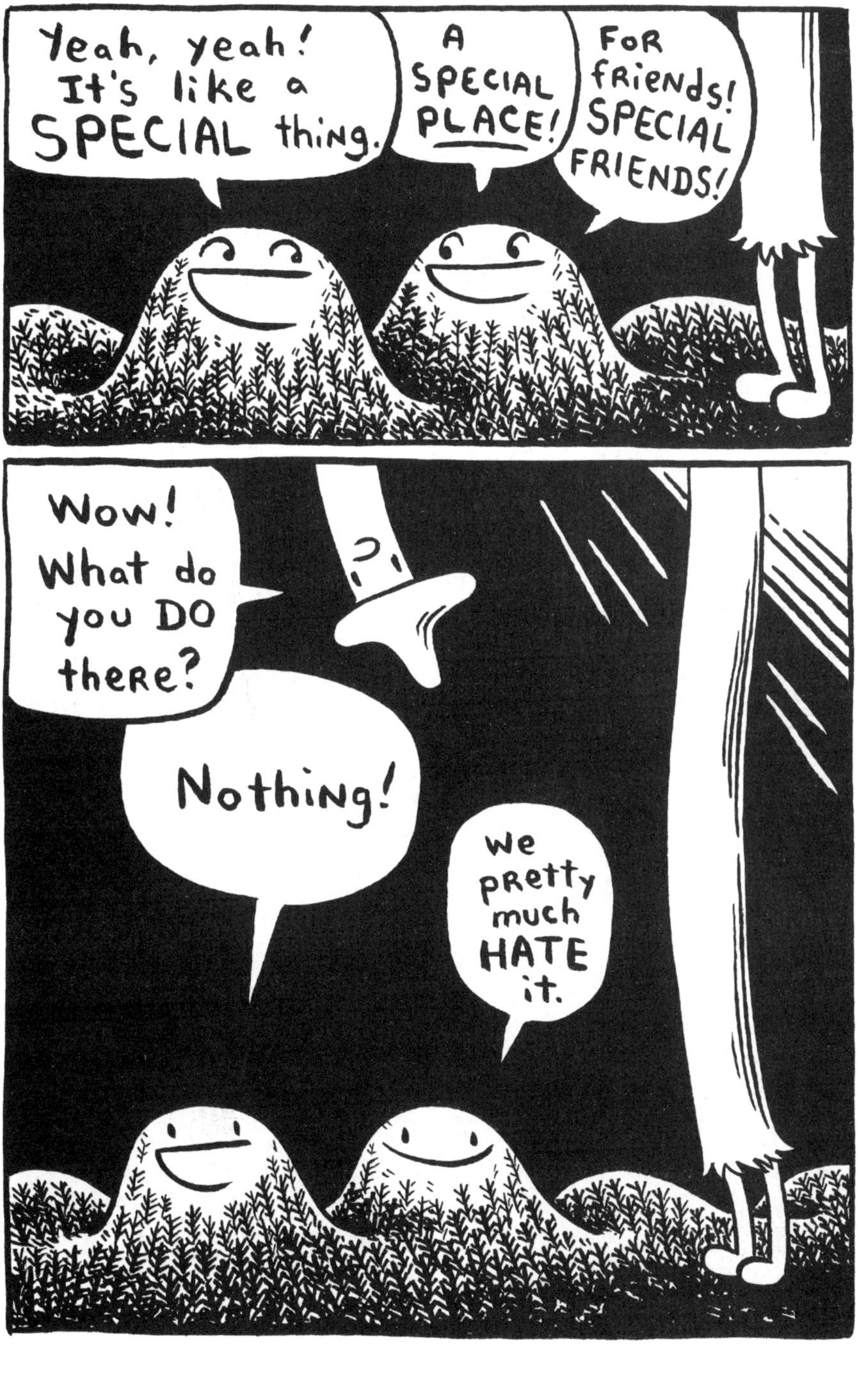
Yeah, yeah! It's like a SPECIAL thing.
A SPECIAL PLACE!
For friends! SPECIAL FRIENDS!
Wow! What do you DO there?
Nothing!
we pretty much HATE it.

Well, okay. Nice. That sounds great. Interesting. Cool. Wow. Yeah.
Thanks for explaining FACEBOOK to me.

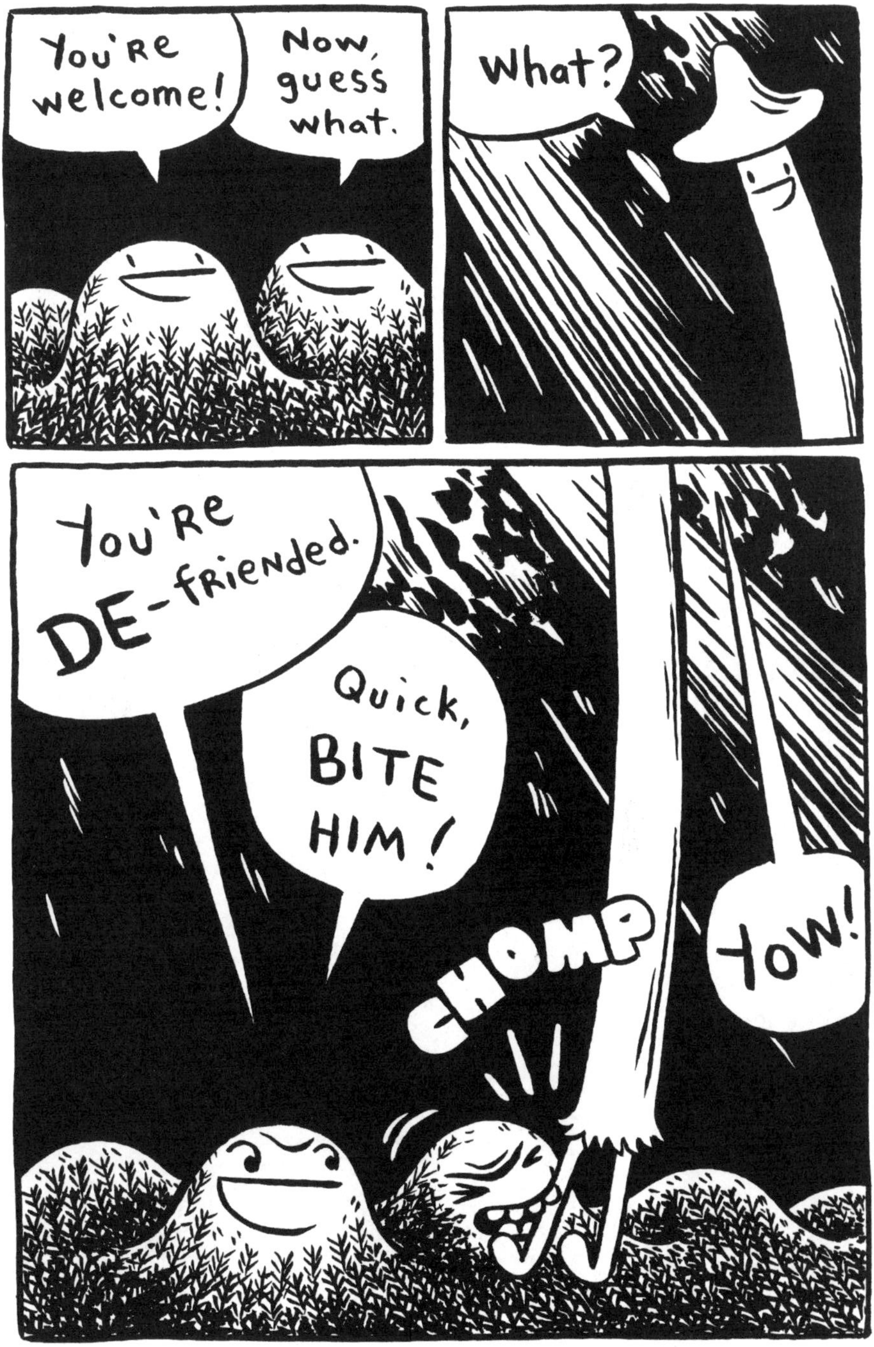
You're welcome!
Now, guess what.
What?
You're DE-friended.
Quick, BITE HIM!
CHOMP
YOW!

Ow! Why did you BITE my lonely foot?
That's PAYBACK!
-for stepping on my FACE.

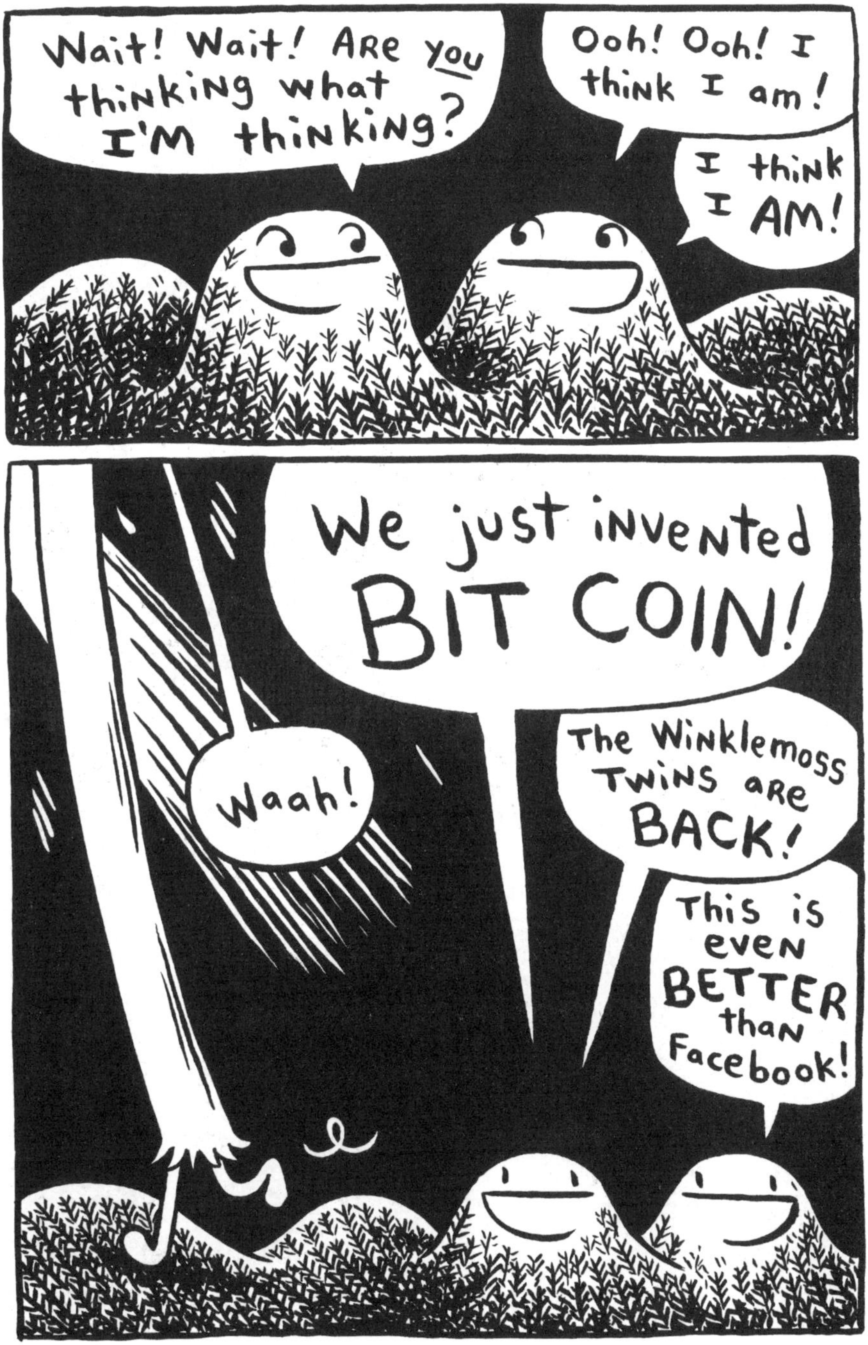
Wait! Wait! ARE you thinking what I'M thinking?
Ooh! Ooh! I think I am!
I think I AM!
We just invented BIT COIN!
Waah!
The Winklemoss TWINS are BACK!
This is even BETTER than Facebook!

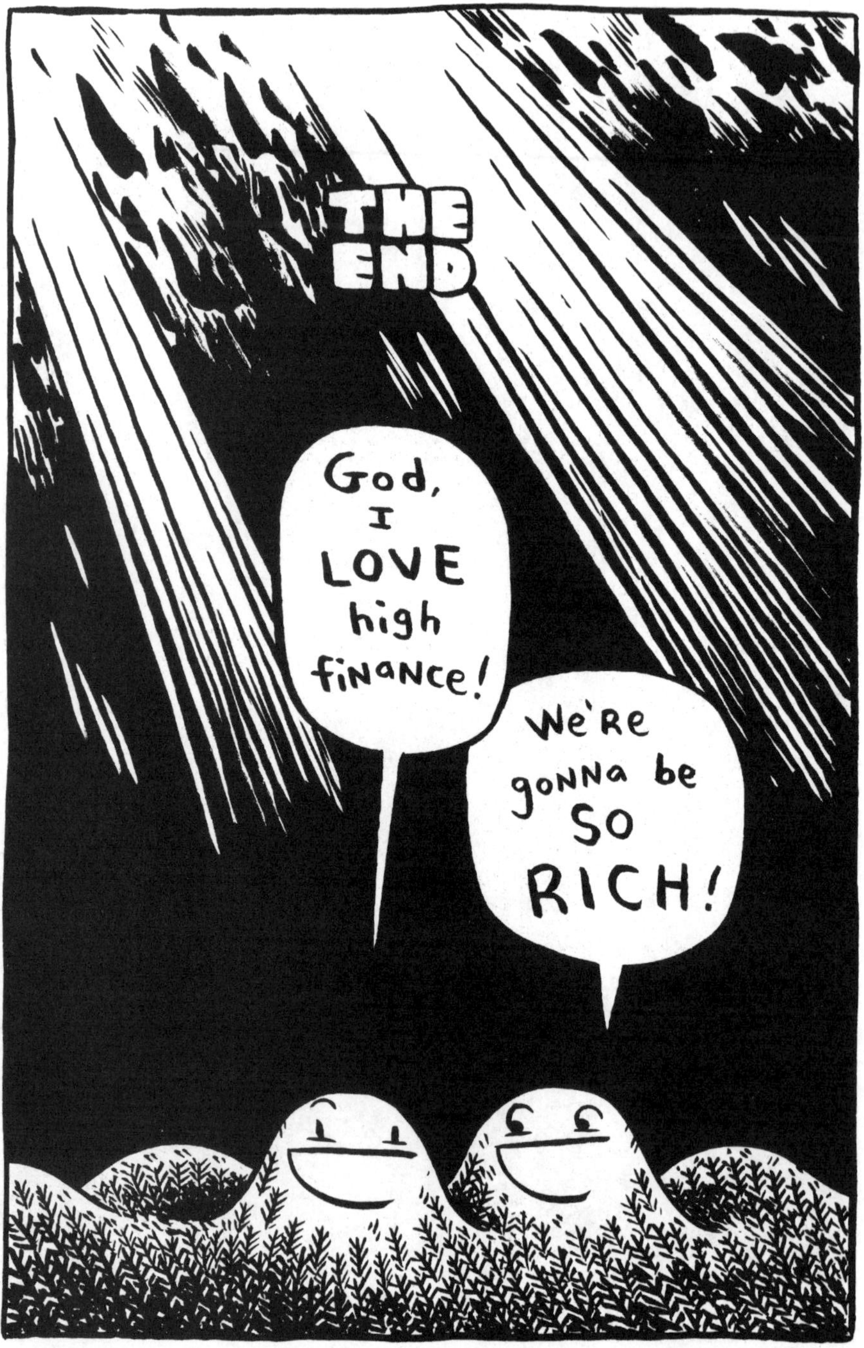
THE END
God, I LOVE high finance!
We're gonna be SO RICH!

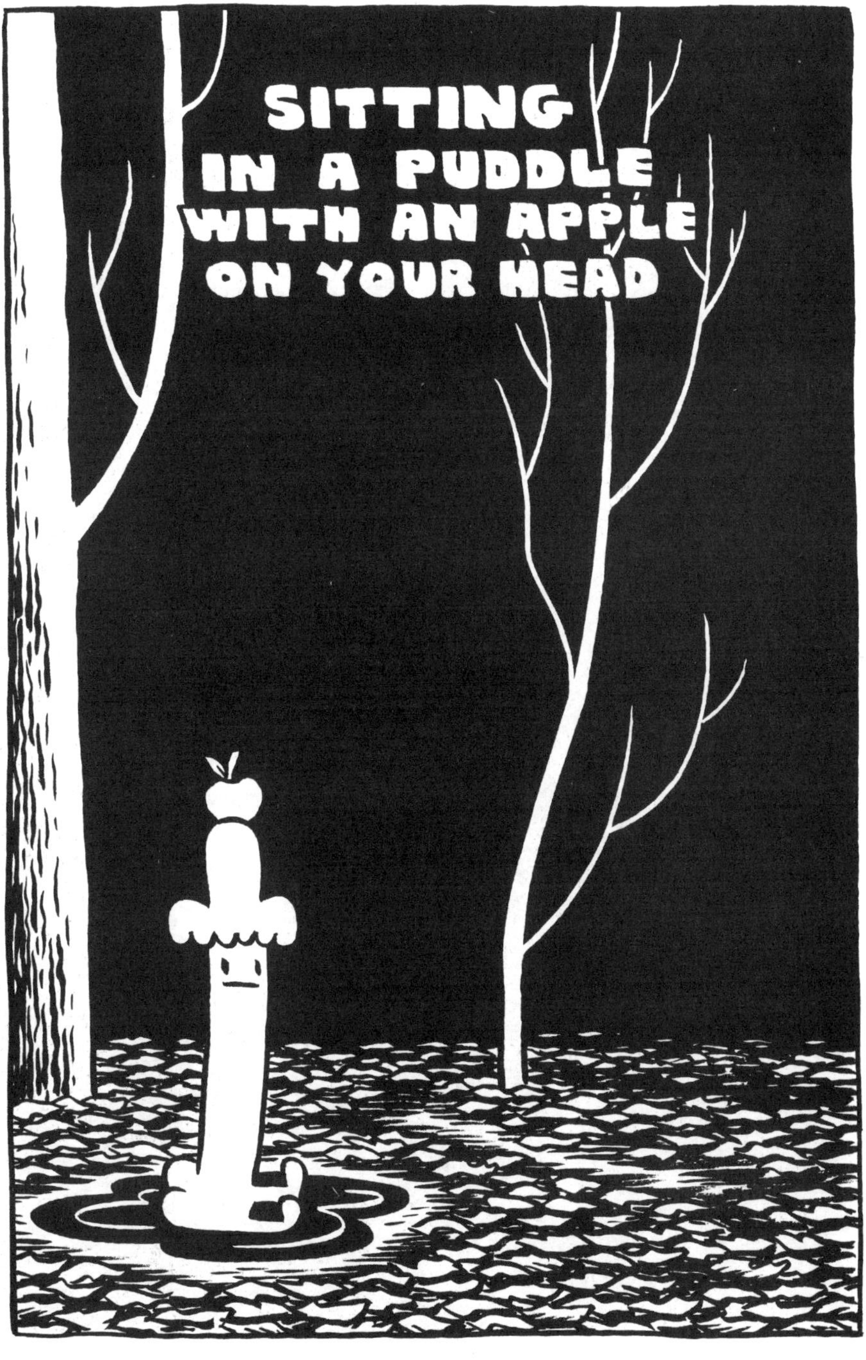
SITTING
IN A PUDDLE
WITH AN APPLE
ON YOUR HEAD

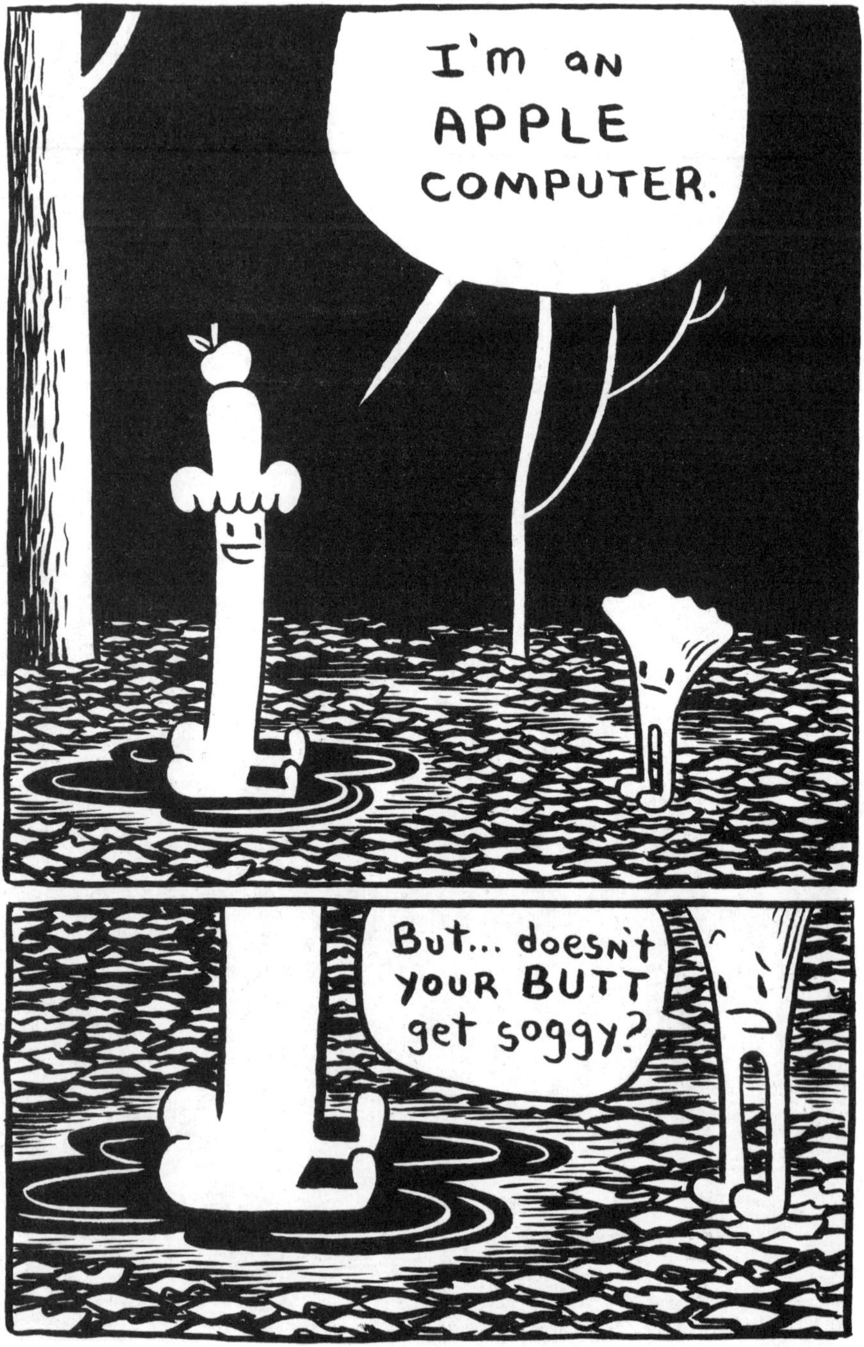
I'm an APPLE COMPUTER.
But... doesn't your BUTT get soggy?

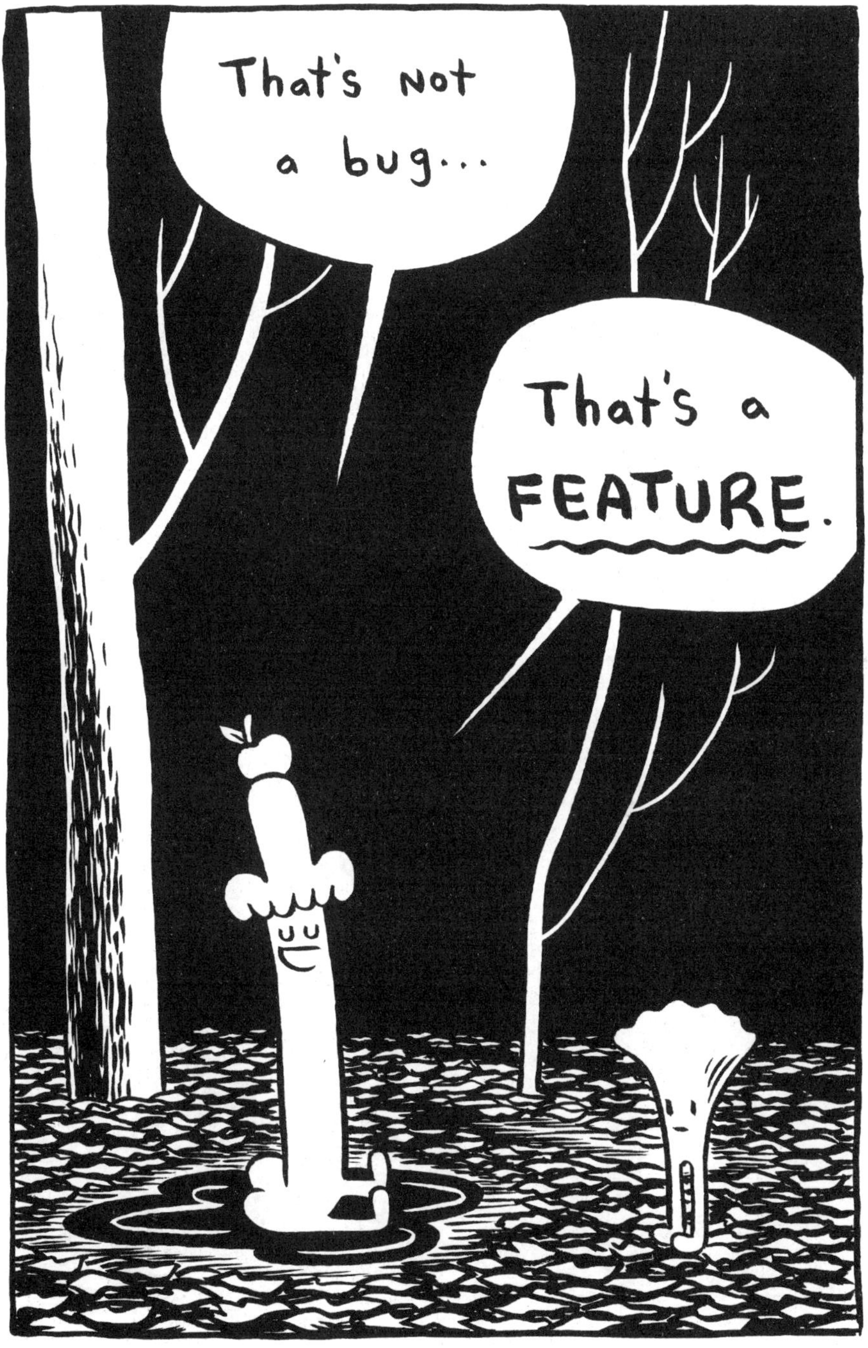
That's not a bug...
That's a FEATURE.

THE END
I guess I'm just about the luckiest boy in the WHOLE WORLD!

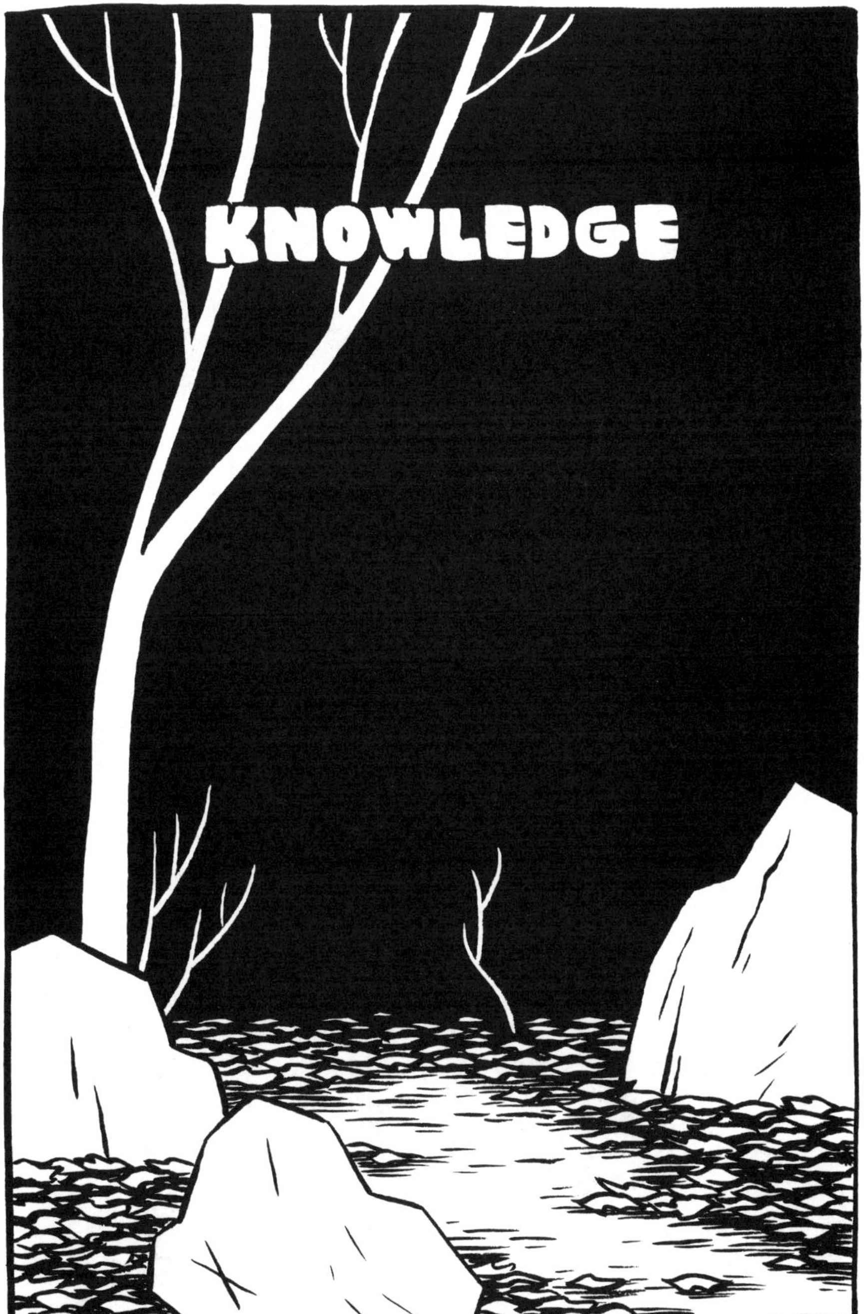
KNOWLEDGE

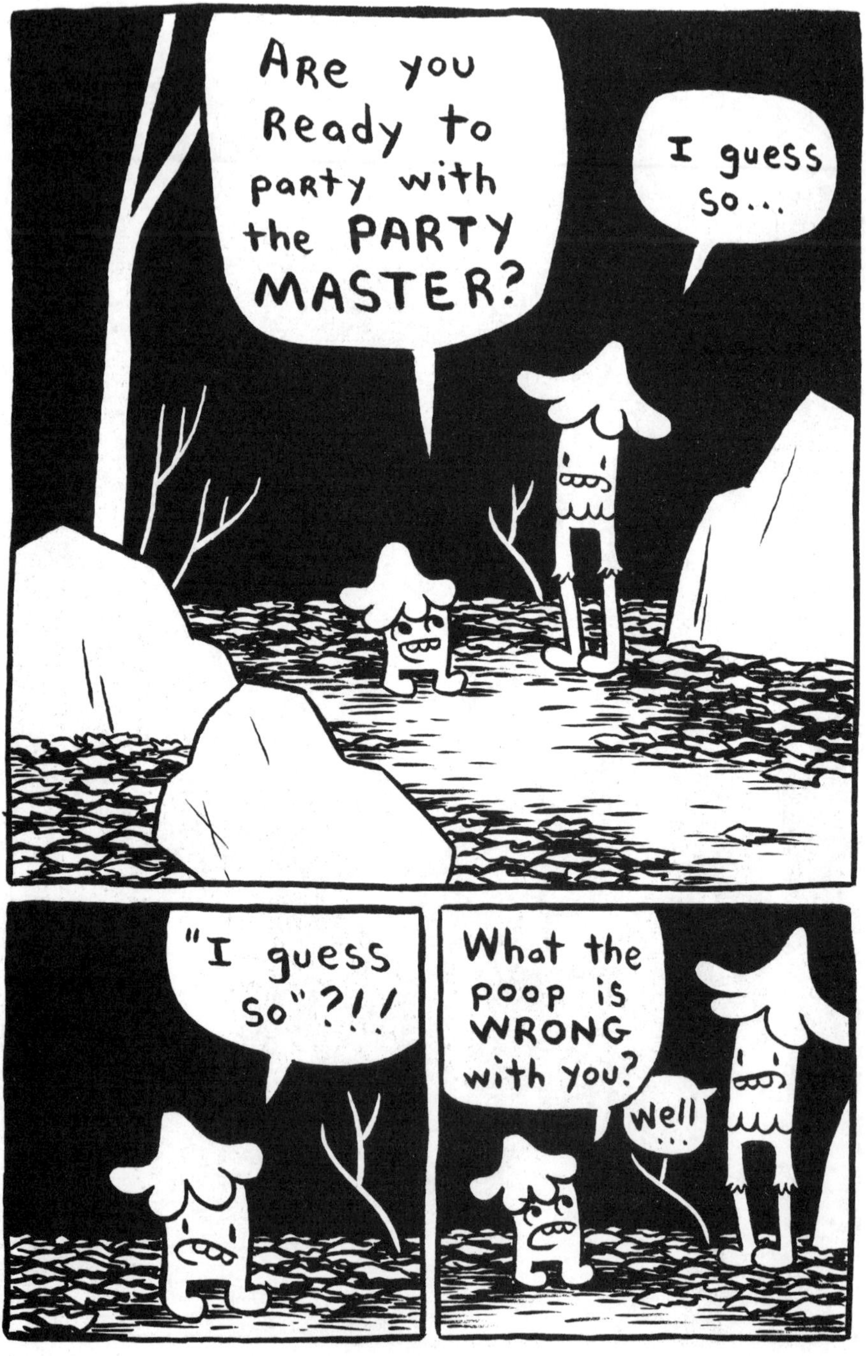
Are you Ready to party with the PARTY MASTER?
I guess so...
"I guess so"?!!
What the poop is WRONG with you?
Well ...

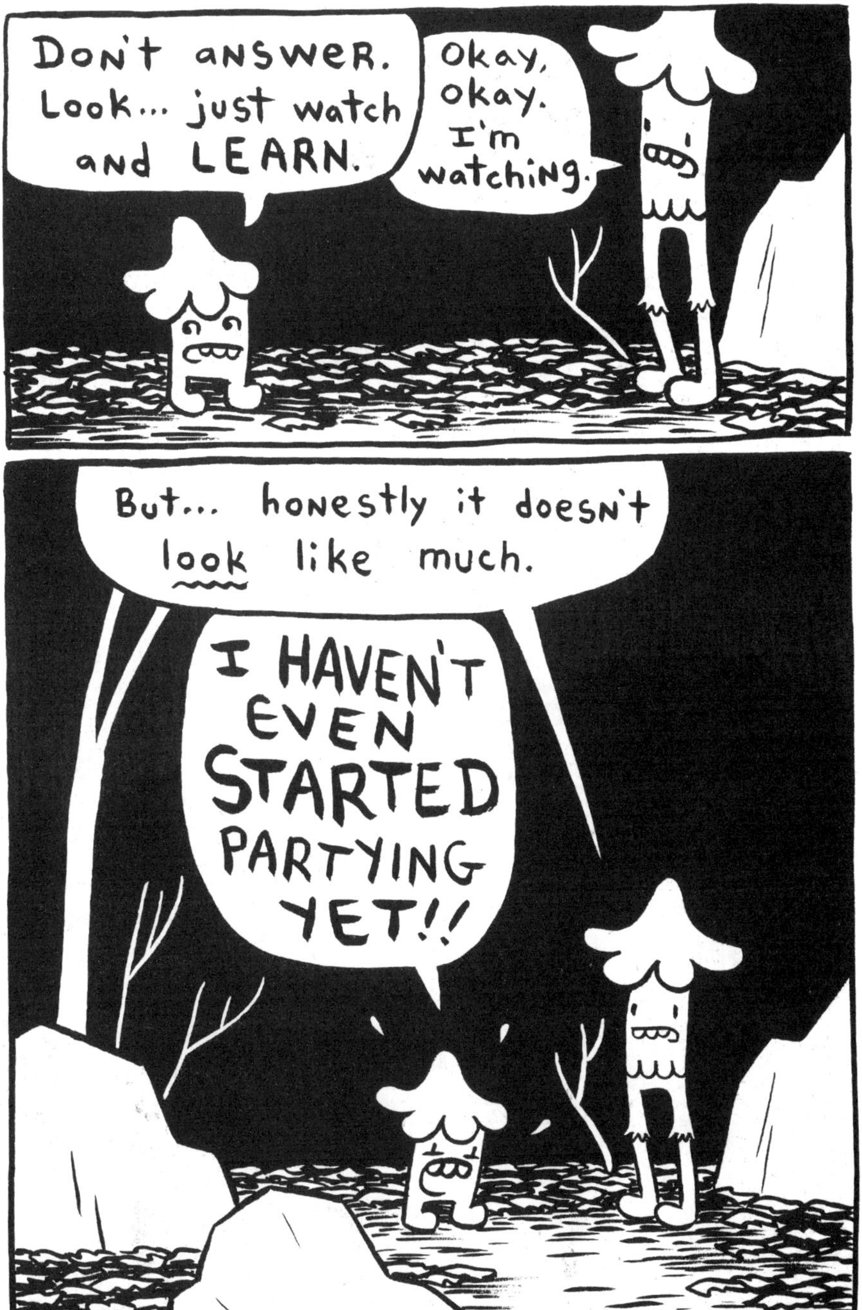
Don't answer. Look... just watch and LEARN.
Okay, okay. I'm watching.
But... honestly it doesn't look like much.
I HAVEN'T EVEN STARTED PARTYING YET!!

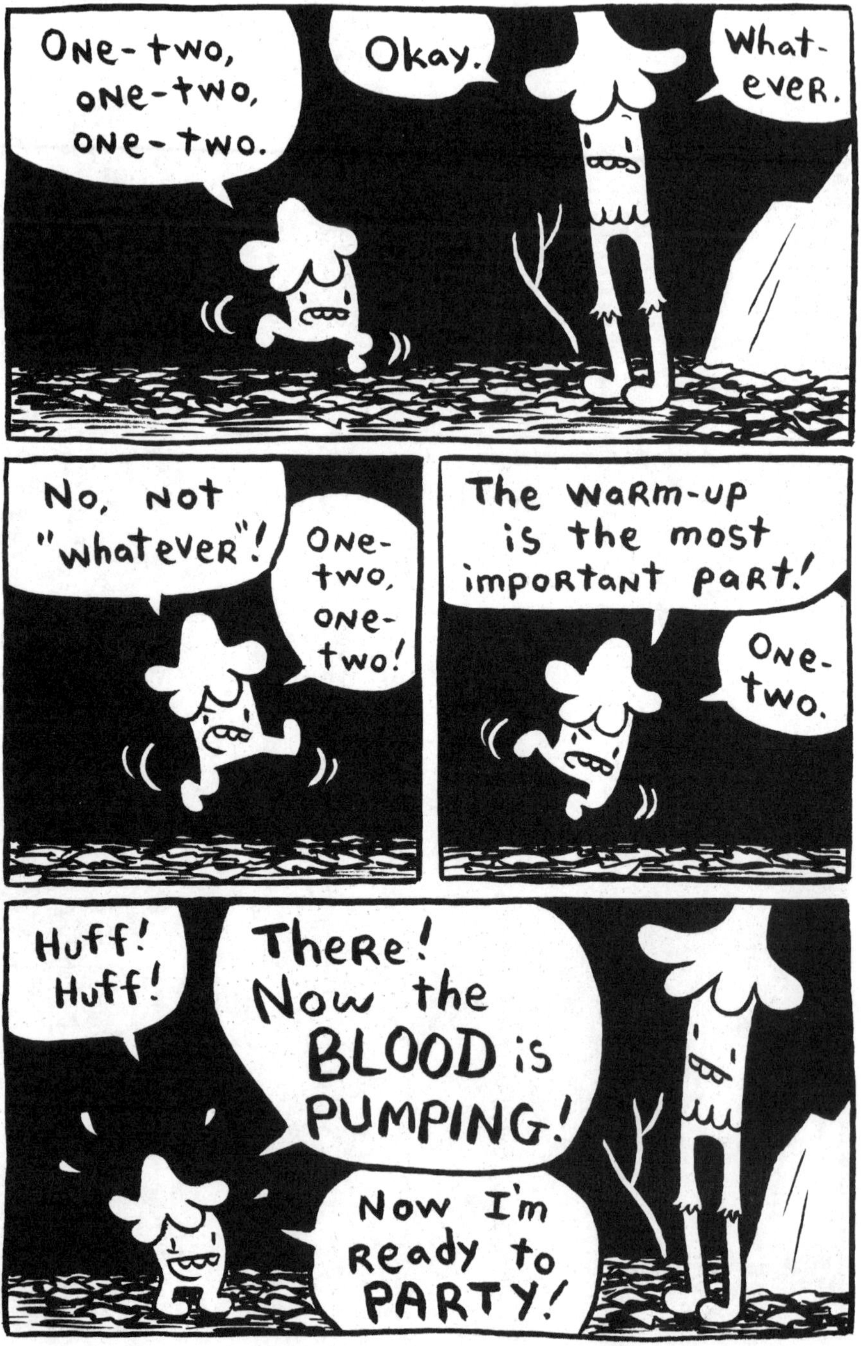
One-two, one-two, one-two.
Okay.
What-ever.
No, not "whatever"!
One-two, one-two!
The warm-up is the most important part!
One-two.
Huff! Huff!
There! Now the BLOOD is PUMPING!
Now I'm ready to PARTY!

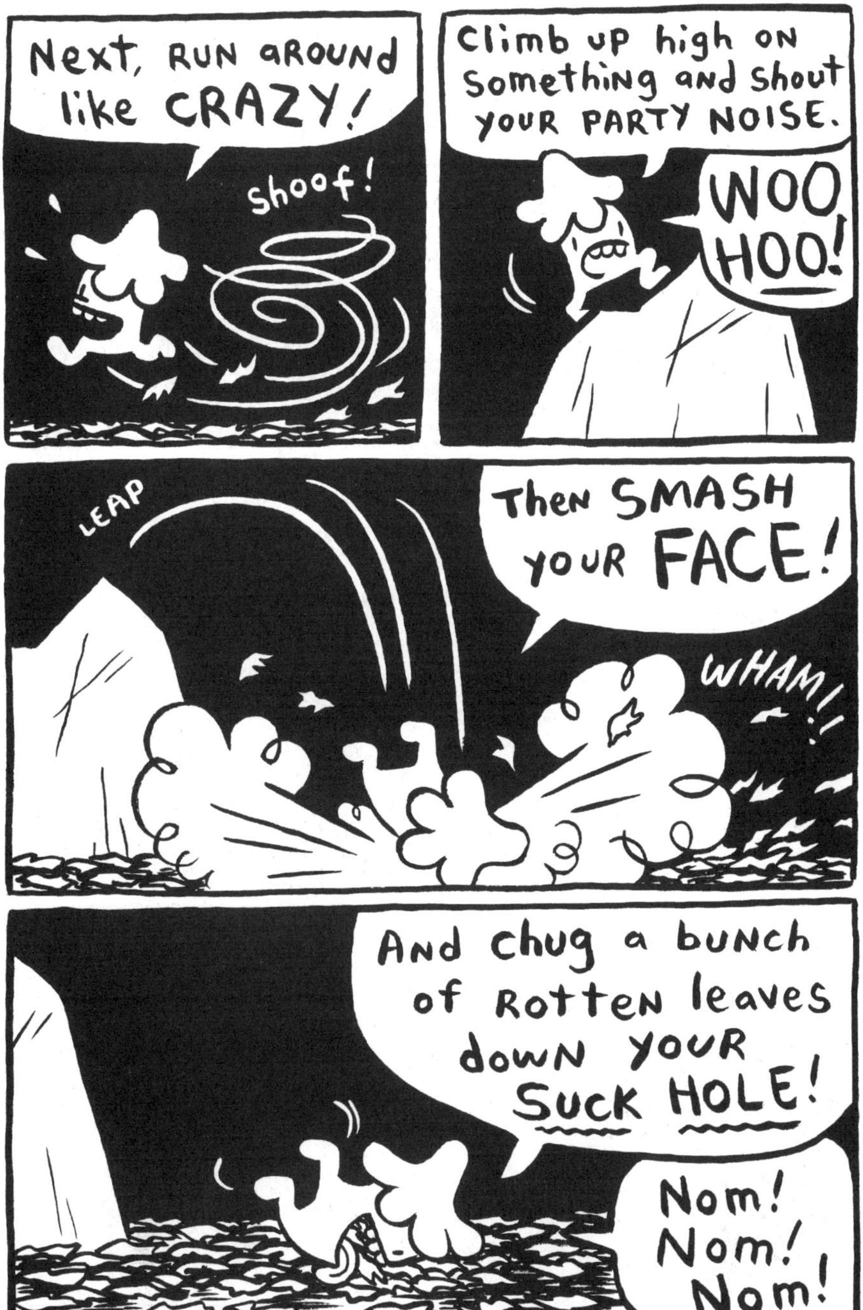

Next, RUN aROUND like CRAZY!
shoof!
Climb up high ON something aNd shout YOUR PARTY NOISE.
WOO HOO!
LEAP
Then SMASH YOUR FACE!
WHAM!!!
ANd chug a buNch of ROtteN leaves dowN YOUR SUCK HOLE!
Nom! Nom! Nom!

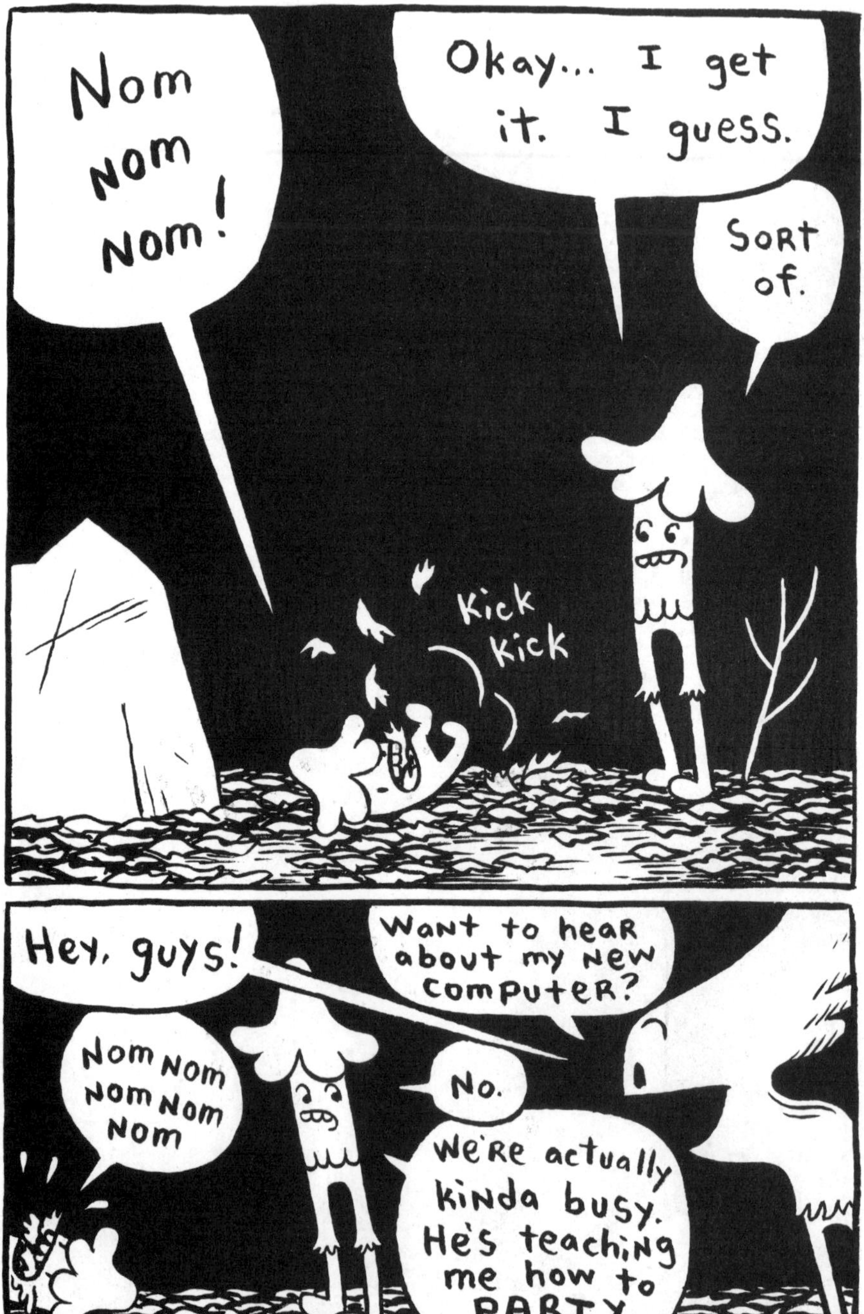
Nom
Nom
Nom!
Okay... I get it. I guess.
Sort of.
Kick
Kick
Hey, guys!
Want to hear about my new computer?
Nom Nom
Nom Nom
Nom
No.
We're actually kinda busy. He's teaching me how to PARTY.

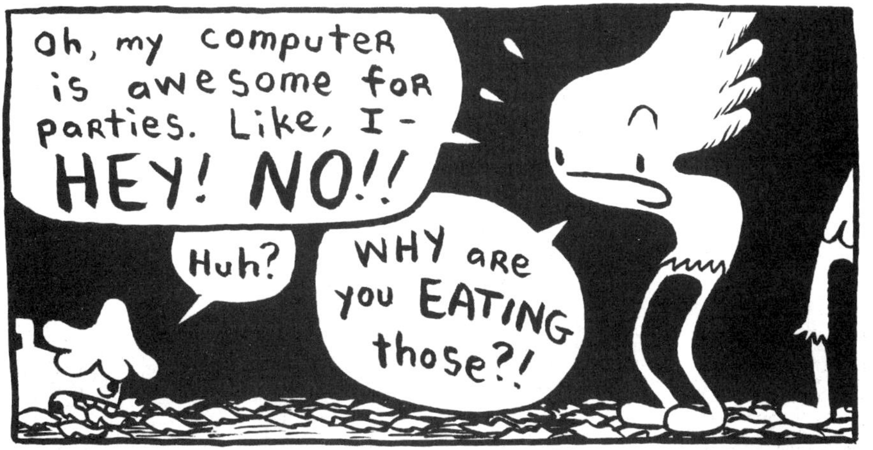
Oh, my computer is awesome for parties. Like, I- HEY! NO!!
Huh?
WHY are you EATING those?!

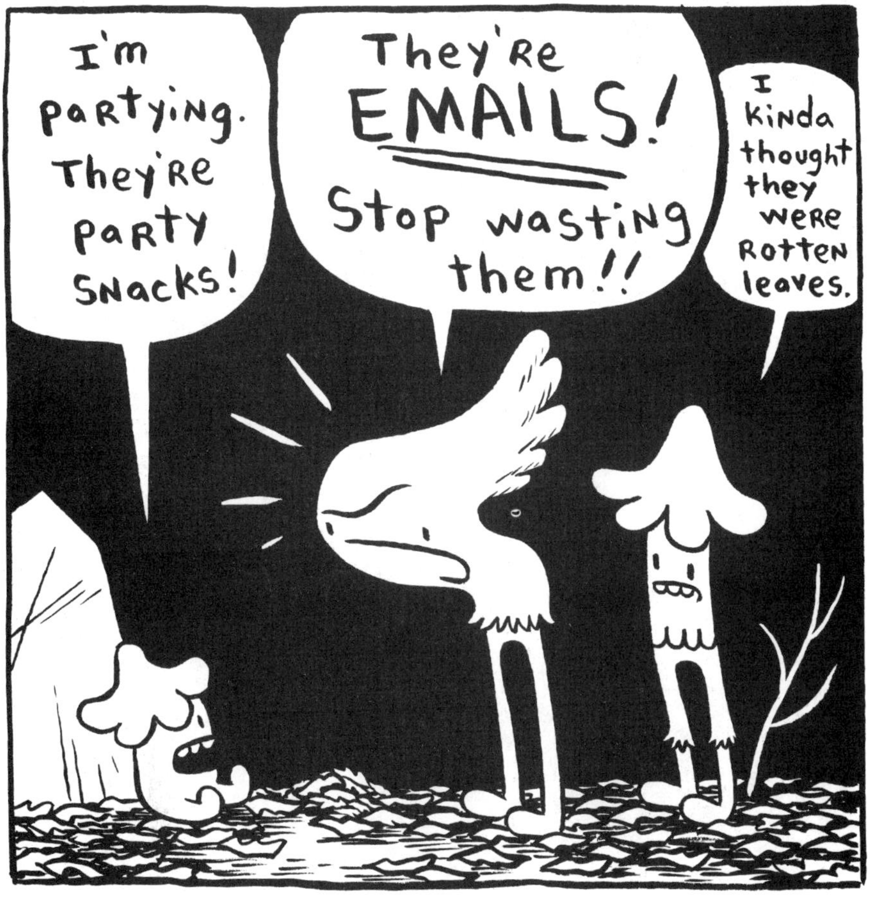
I'm partying. They're party snacks!
They're EMAILS! Stop wasting them!!
I kinda thought they were rotten leaves.

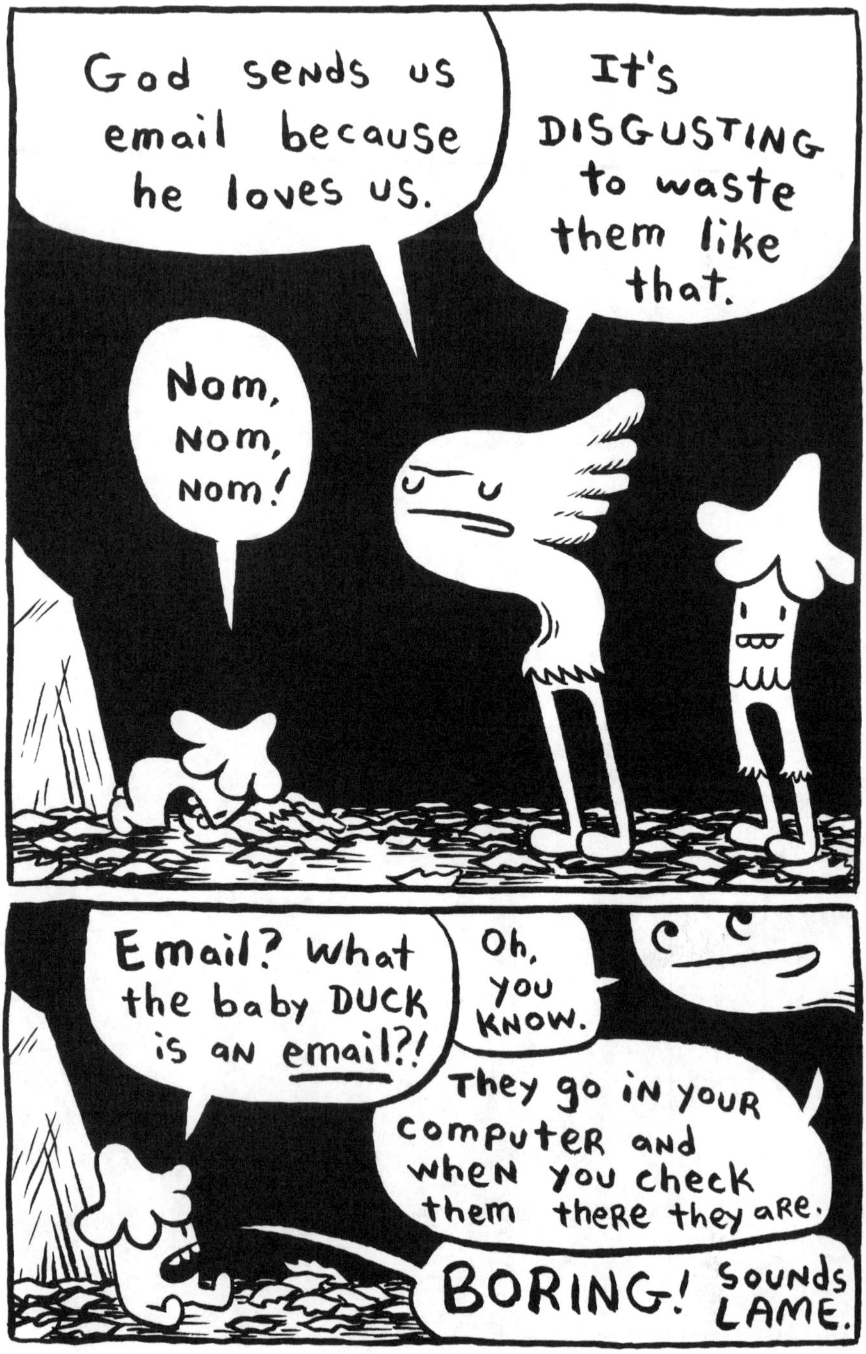
God sends us email because he loves us.
It's DISGUSTING to waste them like that.
Nom, Nom, Nom!
Email? What the baby DUCK is an email?!
Oh, you KNOW.
They go in your computer and when you check them there they are.
BORING! Sounds LAME.

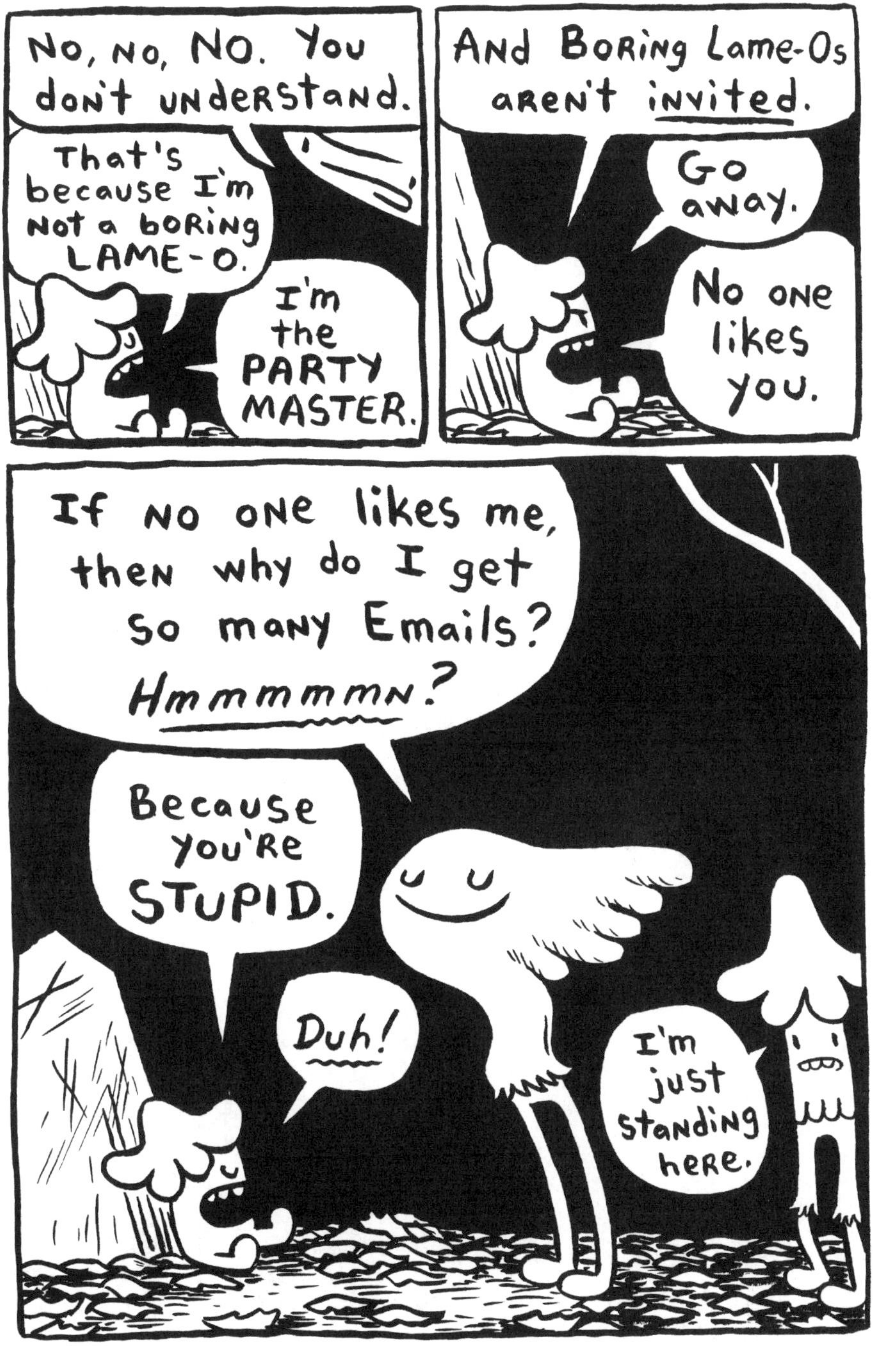
No, no, NO. You don't understand.
That's because I'm not a boring LAME-O.
I'm the PARTY MASTER.
And Boring Lame-Os aren't invited.
Go away.
No one likes you.
If no one likes me, then why do I get so many Emails? Hmmmmmn?
Because you're STUPID.
Duh!
I'm just standing here.

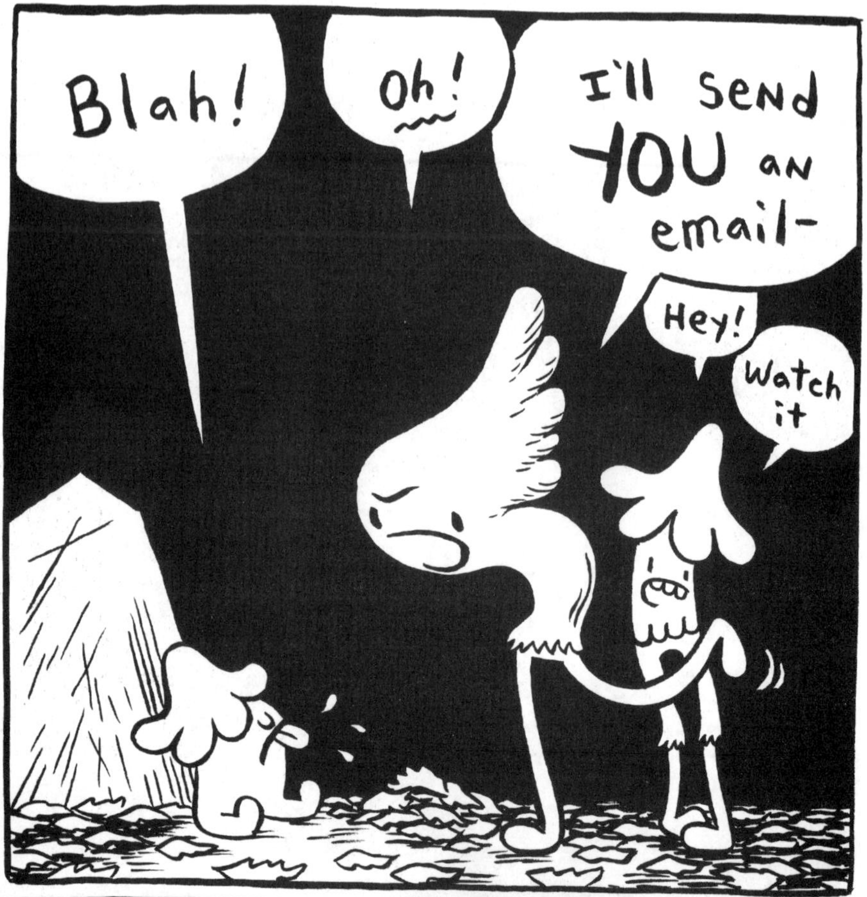
Blah!
Oh!
I'll send YOU an email-
Hey!
Watch it

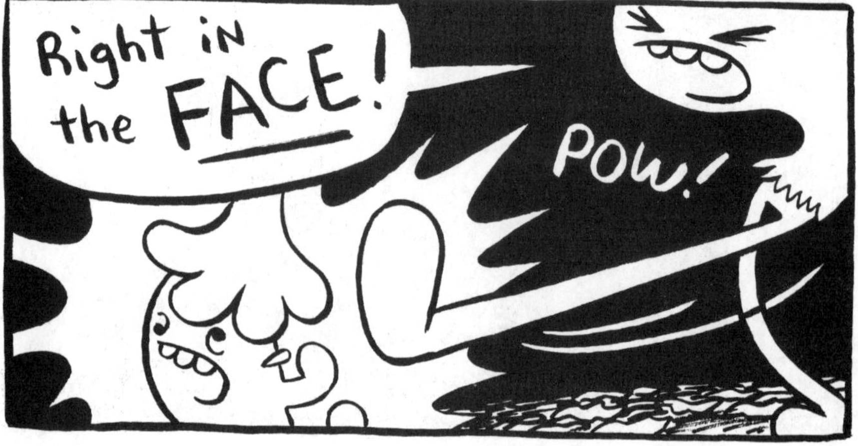
Right in the FACE!
POW!

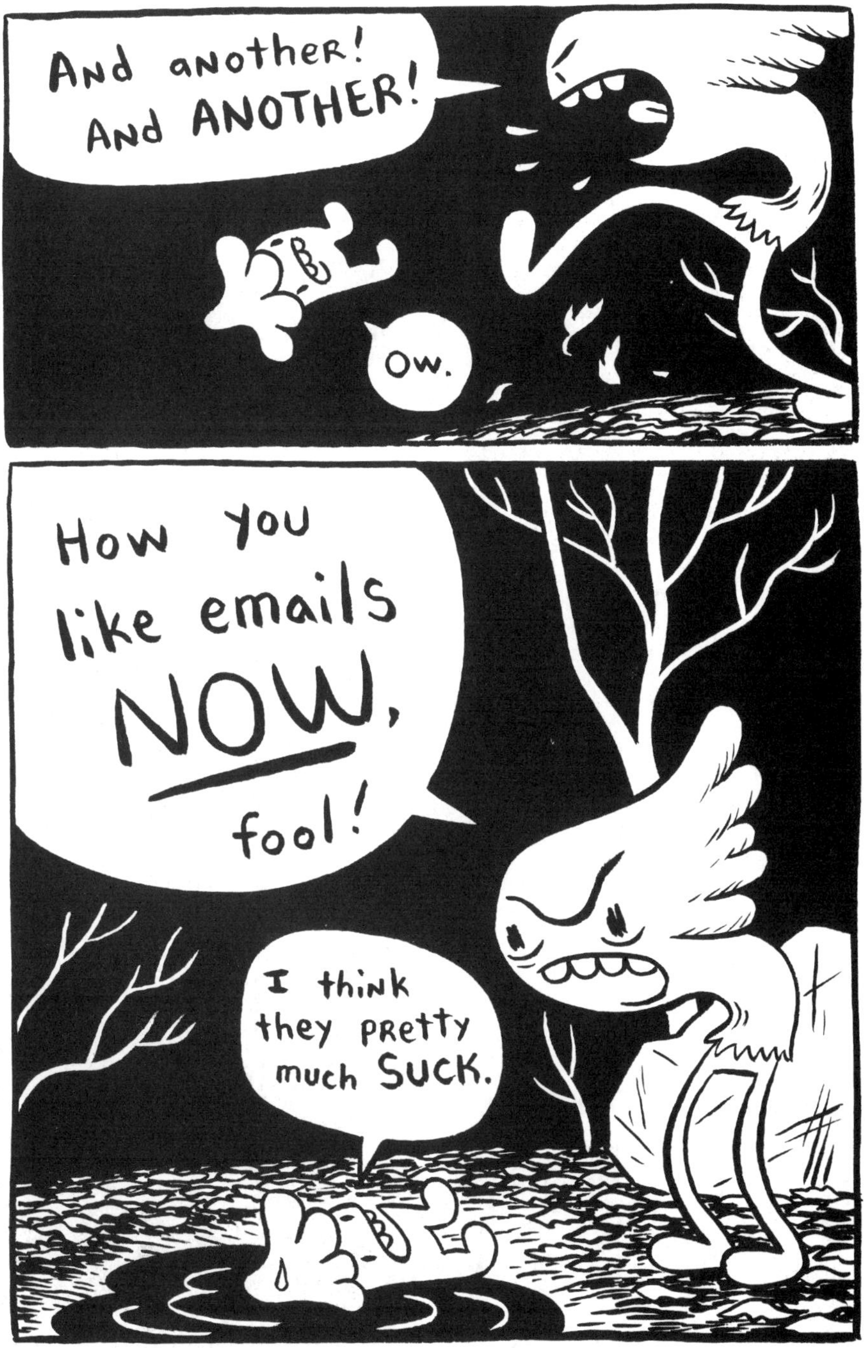
And another! And ANOTHER!
Ow.
How you like emails NOW, fool!
I think they pretty much SUCK.

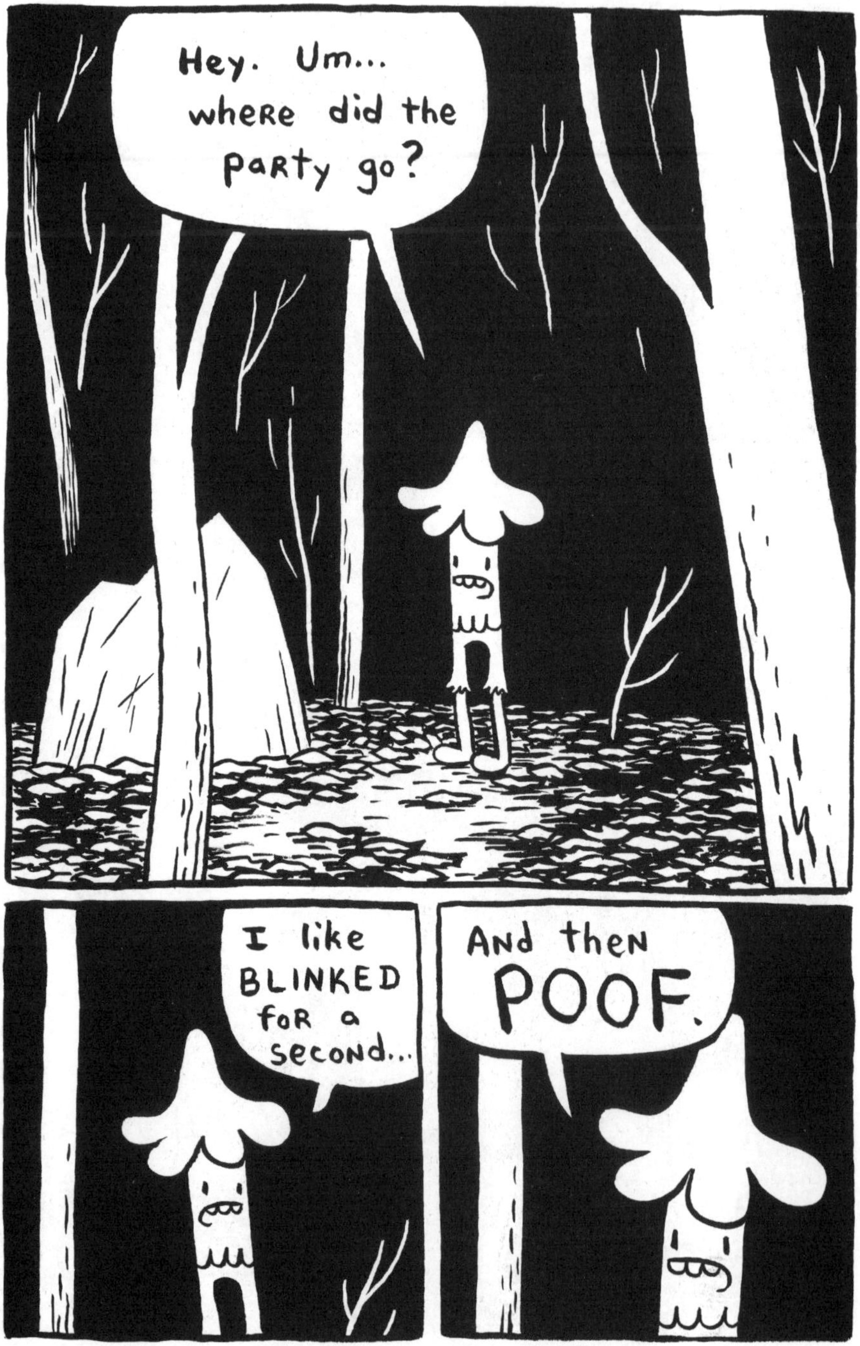
Hey. Um... where did the party go?
I like BLINKED for a second...
And then POOF.

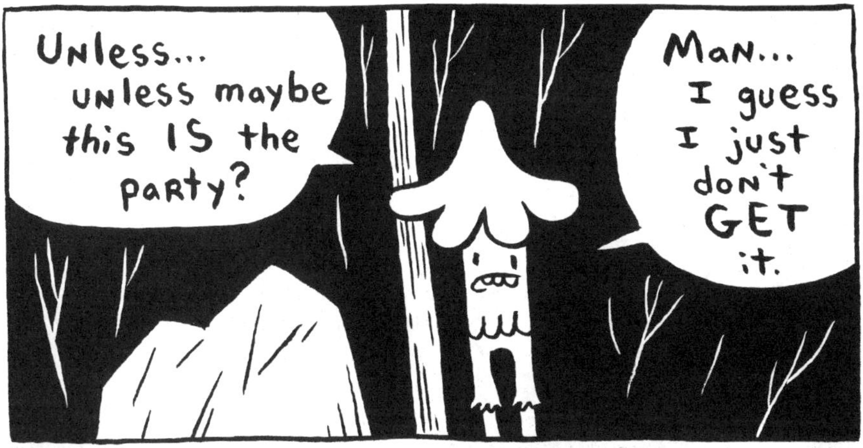
Unless... unless maybe this IS the party?
Man... I guess I just don't GET it.

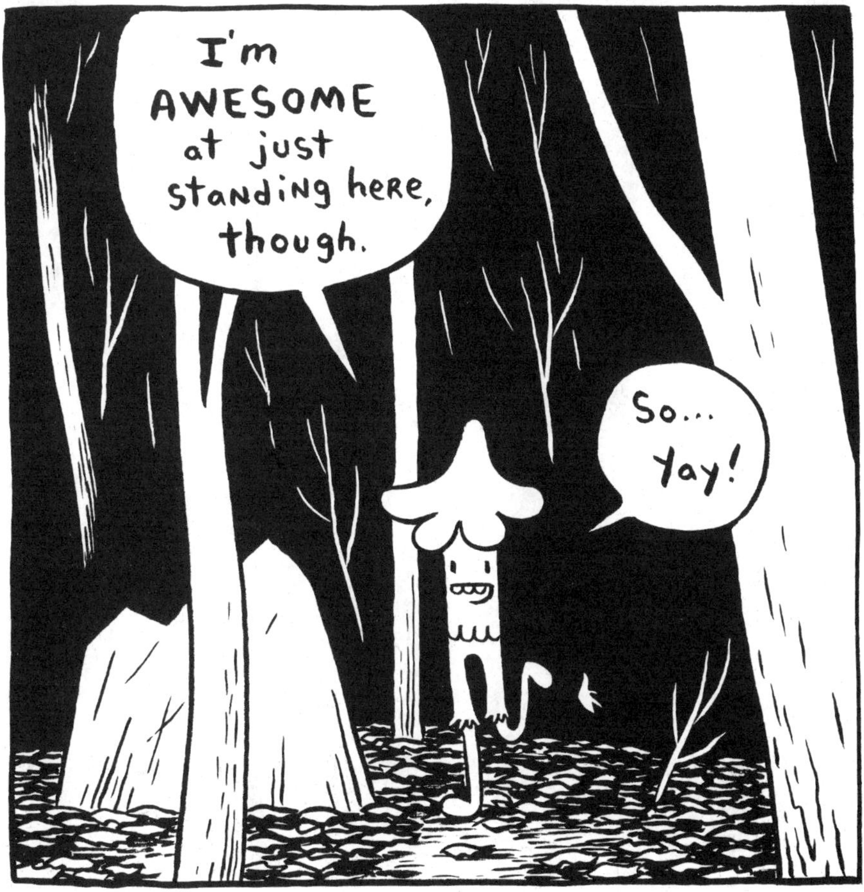
I'm AWESOME at just standing here, though.
So... Yay!

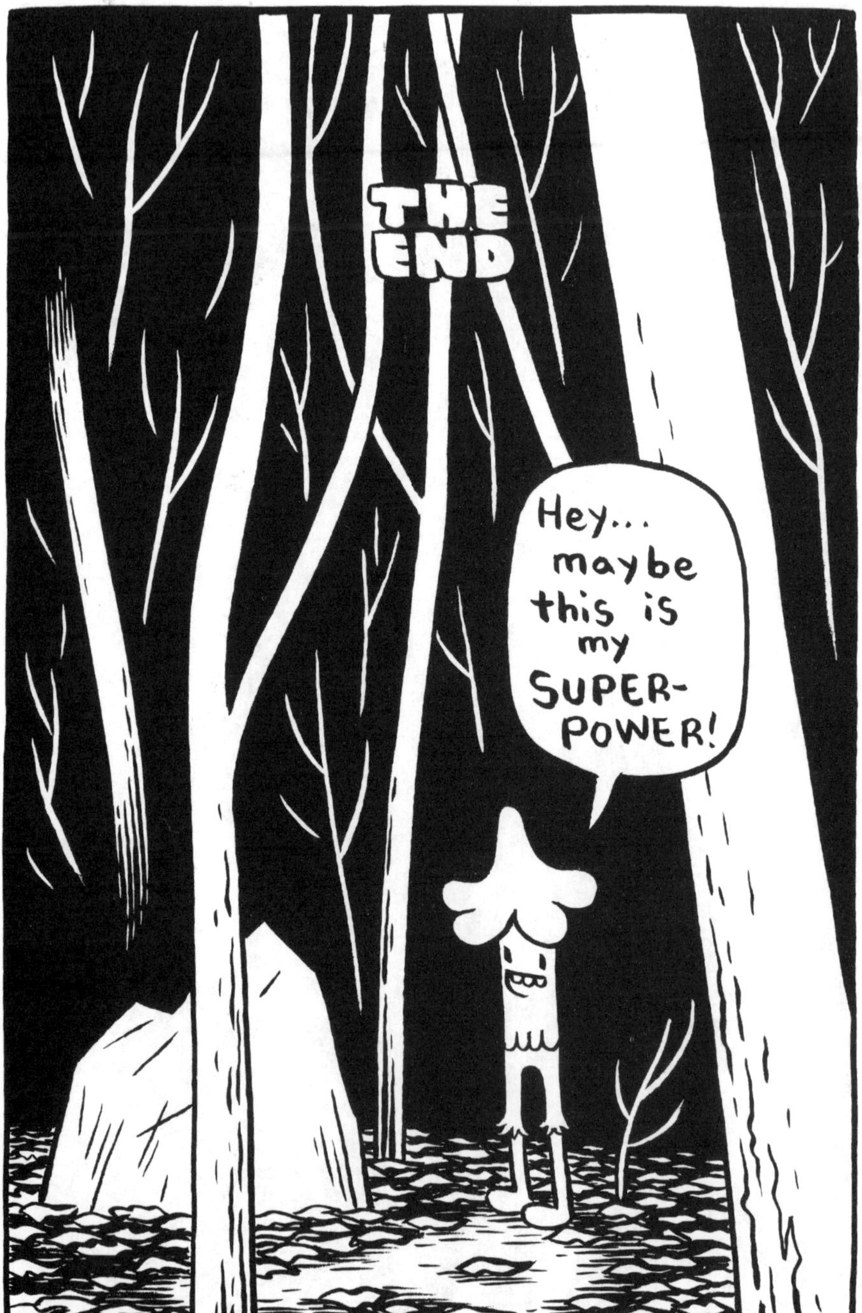
THE END
Hey... maybe this is my SUPER-POWER!

SCAN THIS
QR CODE: